Based on a True Story

Based on a True Story

VIBE SHIFTS, THE END OF DECONSTRUCTION, AND THE REBOOT OF MEANING

PAUL ANLEITNER

NELSON BOOKS
An Imprint of Thomas Nelson

Published by Nelson Books, an imprint of Thomas Nelson, 501 Nelson Place, Nashville, TN 37214, USA. Nelson Books and Thomas Nelson are registered trademarks of HarperCollins Christian Publishing, Inc.

Published in association with the literary agency of WordServe Literary Group, Ltd., www.wordserveliterary.com.

Thomas Nelson titles may be purchased in bulk for educational, business, fundraising, or sales promotional use. For information, please email SpecialMarkets@ThomasNelson.com.

HarperCollins Publishers, Macken House, 39/40 Mayor Street Upper, Dublin 1, D01 C9W8, Ireland (https://www.harpercollins.com)

Library of Congress Cataloging-in-Publication Data

Names: Anleitner, Paul, 1983- author
Title: Based on a true story : vibe shifts, the end of deconstruction, and the reboot of meaning / Paul Anleitner.
Description: Nashville, TN, USA : Nelson Books, [2026] | Includes biographical information. | Includes bibliographical references. | Summary: "Vibe shifts. Religious renaissances. Meaning crises. Movie reboots. "Metamodernism." You listening to Creed again. It's all connected. Cynicism is out, sincerity is back, and there's a new generation looking for hope in unexpected places. We're beginning to find ourselves moving from despair to meaning. As a burned-out culture begins to reject the emptiness of endless deconstruction, people are searching for guidance to rebuild meaning, identity, and community. And believe it or not, your life story and the narrative of our culture are all wrapped up together"-- Provided by publisher.
Identifiers: LCCN 2026009581 (print) | LCCN 2026009582 (ebook) | ISBN 9781400256587 trade paperback | ISBN 9781400257034 ebook
Subjects: LCSH: Spirituality--United States--History--21st century | Religion and culture--United States--History--21st century | Popular culture--United States--History--21st century
Classification: LCC BL624 .A55 2026 (print) | LCC BL624 (ebook)
LC record available at https://lccn.loc.gov/2026009581
LC ebook record available at https://lccn.loc.gov/2026009582

Art direction: Curt Diepenhorst
Cover design: Tim Green, Tiny Giant Co
Interior design: Sara Guild

Printed in the United States of America

26 27 28 29 30 LBC 5 4 3 2 1

Contents

Foreword

What is a "you"?

I know it sounds like something your college roommate pesters you with at 3 a.m. after they've engaged in some form of contraband activity. But I'm stone-cold sober here. What kind of thing constitutes a "you"?

Are you your body—ribbons of tissue, organs, and bones? Are you your face, your fingers, your toes? What about your nails? When you get a haircut, have you left a pile of "you" on the floor? If it ever *was* you, how come it isn't you anymore?

Are you just your cells? They regenerate, you know. You are also, and possibly more so, an unseen force of life and will that propels your fluctuating, regenerating clusters of cells through space.

Some would call that unseen force a *story*.

Paul and I became friends several years ago, around the time my own script had led me into a bit of a dark cul-de-sac. He was one of several voices that served as a guiding light in that season as I felt my way back to the path of faith and meaning.

During that time, I noticed he had a unique gift for seeing the programs that run beneath the surface of our cultural moment. I might even call it a gift of discernment. We had long, fascinating conversations about what films, songs, and even comic books were *really* telling us about the world we lived in and where it was all headed. Sometimes he would make wild, even hilarious, predictions, and—I kid you not—sometimes they would happen just as he said. (I'm sure it surprised him as much as the rest of us.)

One day not long ago, he called me to say he felt like a change was coming. I could hear a palpable joy in his voice as he swore the world was ready to relinquish some of the nihilism, cynicism, and dismissive irony that held a stranglehold on our cultural landscape. There's a changing of the guard, he told me, and maybe it's our time to step up and be a part of it. Maybe it's on us to till the narrative soil from which our children can grow a better world. So, what if we put our energy into building things instead of tearing them apart?

Deep down in my bones, I knew he was right. It's time to grow gardens instead of lighting dumpster fires. It's time to make something beautiful and generative together. And it all starts by answering the most important question about who we are in the world.

Because at the heart of every person is a hidden narrative, a unique web of fears and desires that lean on every material choice they make. Over time, the real-world consequences of these choices form us into the creatures we become. We make stories. We are made of stories.

I'm sure it's more complicated than that, and I won't attempt to perform any metaphysics here, especially here at the beginning of my friend Paul's book. Still, in my humble opinion, if that's only a metaphor, it's *barely* only a metaphor.

Applied at scale, it's not difficult to see how these stories shape history, as civilizations rise and fall on unseen ideas, ideals, and ideologies. And it's unsettling when you stop to consider who's usually writing the script. Just think about who benefits from it. (Spoiler alert: It's usually not you.) What a revelation to realize that we're allowed to tell ourselves a better story.

So, what's *your* story?

John Mark McMillan

Prologue

As a child of the 1980s and '90s, I often feel like I was born into a world between worlds. We didn't have the internet in my house until I was in college. We relied on physical maps or the wisdom of gas station attendants to locate any destination outside our daily commute. The hostess at the local Big Boy restaurant would ask if my parents, along with my three younger siblings and me, would like to sit in the smoking section next to those patrons who enjoyed pairing their pancakes with a pack of Marlboros or in the nonsmoking section, where it was somehow magically impossible to be poisoned by the gray cloud of nicotine and tar-flavored cigarette fumes just three tables away.

Much has changed since those days. It's not just the existence of the internet and social media or the fact that a guy can't light up a heater in the corner booth with his kids anymore. When I was a child, 6 percent of Americans claimed to have no religious affiliation.[1] By the time I was an adult, nearly one quarter of all adults were *nones*.[2] The church pews kept emptying, and eventually there were more nones than evangelicals, the second largest Christian demographic in the US. Though challenges to faith have existed for every generation, why did the greatest loss of faith in American history happen during my lifetime?[3]

It's not just that the pews were rapidly emptying. Call it a feeling or a *vibe* or whatever, but something was definitively changing in American culture as I got older. As you'll see in the opening chapter, there was something different about the stories we were starting to tell about ourselves, the world, and the point of life . . . if there even was a point. With this shift came an unprecedented epidemic of cynicism, spiritual homelessness, and despair.

From the start of the new millennium to the end of the 2010s, deaths from suicide increased 35 percent.[4] Drug-overdose deaths increased five-fold.[5] People who wanted to be freed from this despair seemed less certain of where to turn for help. Americans' trust in every major institution of our society—government, media, and even church—declined all at the same time.[6]

Sometime in the mid-2010s, a new term to describe the cultural moment began floating around the internet: the *meaning crisis*. Popularized by my friend John Vervaeke, a cognitive scientist and philosopher at the University of Toronto, it attempted to describe the growing awareness that this culture-wide feeling of cynicism, loneliness, and nihilism had become an epidemic. Concerns began to mount that if we did not address this meaning crisis, it might lead—quite literally—to the end of civilization, no matter if we could eventually build rockets to Mars or artificially intelligent robots to fold our laundry.

As we'll see in the pages ahead, every generation is shaped by the stories their culture tells them. My generation was formed by an *anti-story* about how the highest good in life was to be a revolutionary rebel, raging against the machine and *seeing through* every lie of the past in the inevitable march of progress. But a quiet dissatisfaction was brewing inside us. Everyone had a deconstruction tale to tell; even more had a podcast about it. If this was progress, why wasn't our meaning crisis going away?

As a friend growing weary with his own deconstruction confessed to me, "I'd get together with my friends who were deconstructing, and all we'd do together is rail against everything we saw wrong with the world. Whoever was the most cynical and the most ironic got the most status, but then I would go home and feel worse than before." Living in that anti-story, while knowing only what he should be against, wasn't working. My friend's longing for meaning sent him searching for a better story.

He wasn't alone.

Like the poet Christian Wiman, who penned the lament "All My Friends Are Finding New Beliefs," I had watched so many friends drift from one project of discontent to the next. We couldn't live without meaning, so we went to therapy, dabbled with some do-it-yourself spiritualities, and maybe even tried a little ayahuasca with a shaman down in the Amazon; yet despair lingered on, and visions of a civilizational collision course with a dystopian *Mad Max* future still haunted our dreams.

Then, rather quite suddenly, the cultural vibe shifted again. Headlines began to read, "Young Adults Lead a Resurgence in Church Attendance,"[7] and "New Data Shows Gen Z Men Returning to Church." When one young man was interviewed about why this was happening, he replied, "I think Gen Z is looking for meaning."[8] This surprising religious reversal would be sufficiently fascinating if it were the lone marker of the cultural shift, but it isn't.

Artists and filmmakers, exhausted by decades of detached irony, began experimenting with an antidote to cynicism: sincerity. People tired of always feeling just six feet from the edge of overwhelming despair began to crank Y2K-era power ballads in their cars, hoping to find a wholesome feeling that seemed lost to time. Who cares if it had been deemed "cringe" for twenty years? A new cultural mantra was emerging for those ready to give hope another shot, even if it wasn't cool: *Embrace the cringe.*

The spiritual *closedness* of the last few decades was giving way to a post-cynical wave of *openness.* We bottomed out in our meaning crisis and came face-to-face with an apocalypse, but a return to meaning is now on the horizon. And you might be surprised at the places where you can find it. I'm going to show you other signs of the times, why they are happening, and what they mean. I bet you've already noticed some sightings yourself over these last few years.

By the end of your journey through this book, I hope that you'll not only understand the signs of the times but realize that you have a role to play in the greatest story ever told. We are at a critical pivot point living in a world between worlds, where a historic opportunity for cultural renewal is before us. What kind of world will our children and grandchildren inherit? The answer to that question depends on what we do with this moment.

It's time to rebuild.

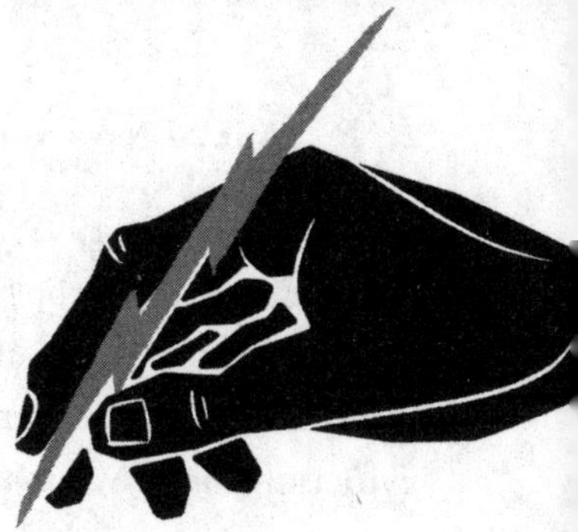

CHAPTER 1

Break Stuff: A Culture in Collapse

> Your head will collapse
> But there's nothing in it.
> *The Pixies, "Where Is My Mind?"*

The dissonant notes of a guitar bellow over the backbeat of *boom-boom-bop, boom-boom-bop* on the drums. A ghostly falsetto howl, soaked in reverb, slides over and over between two notes. The singer strains to hit the notes, which seem slightly flat due to some aesthetic choice. The soundtrack accompanies a scene of a city skyline erupting into flames backdropped against a night sky. In the barely lit foreground, a man and woman stand hand in hand, taking in the view of each building exploding in erratic sequence.

The man has the blood of a self-inflicted gunshot wound pouring from his face and neck. He, or perhaps more accurately, *some part of himself*, orchestrated the destruction of the city's financial buildings, organizing a band of disenfranchised men to turn their despair into a project of mayhem. The couple takes one final look at each other as the city lights begin to dim, and the screen fades to black.

The year was 1999, and I was sixteen years old when I sat through my first viewing of the final scene of the cult hit *Fight Club*. Raised in a devout Christian family, I had no business watching that movie with its brutal violence bordering on sadomasochism paired with unrelenting cynicism (sorry, Mom and Dad, if you're just now finding this out). I remember feeling a heaviness as I watched it. And yet there was something seductively alluring about its irony, cynicism, anti-consumerism, and anti-establishment message. Edward Norton's nameless character, sitting through his soul-sucking office job, with the film's color palette washed out by a dull, depressing shade of green, portrayed a future I wanted no part of when I stepped into adulthood.

In that same year another cult phenomenon, featuring yet another disgruntled man enduring a miserable office job and filmed in the same color palette as *Fight Club*'s office scenes, called on viewers to consider the first cultural instantiation of the term *red-pilled*. Morpheus, a countercultural Obi-Wan Kenobi for the new postmodern moment, reached out his hands and invited Keanu Reeves's character, Neo, to make a choice. If he took the blue pill, he would remain a naive, docile sheep and go back to his prison cell of an office cubicle. If he took the red pill, he would wake up to the reality that he was a slave to the system. "Like everyone else, you were born into bondage, born into a prison that you cannot smell or taste or touch."[1]

To the millions who saw *Fight Club* and *The Matrix*, the message of these parables was clear: The world you were born into is a sham. Society has failed you. Spark a revolution to overthrow the system and burn it to the ground.

That summer, Woodstock ended in a literal fire-and-brimstone scene that looked not altogether different from the end of *Fight Club*. Angst and violence began to brew on the penultimate evening of Woodstock '99 as the nu-metal rap-rock band Limp Bizkit started to play their hit song "Break Stuff." The next day at the culmination of this music festival that had been branded as the peace-and-love revival of the original Woodstock of 1969, fires began to break out. Hordes of young people, caught up in a state of frenzy, stormed throughout the festival fairgrounds looting vendors, tearing down massive speaker towers, and setting fire to property, vehicles, and semitrailers.

Festival participants described how crowds roving from one scene of chaos to the next chanted the infamous tagline to Rage Against the Machine's "Killing in the Name": "[Bleep] you, I won't do what you tell me!" If you've ever seen pictures of the aftermath, then you'll know that it's not hyperbole to say that the rubble and ash of Woodstock '99 looked like a foreign war zone on the evening news.

Something had shifted in American popular culture in the 1990s. A seismic spiritual change had been brewing among academia and the high culture of the educated intelligentsia for some time, but only now was it beginning to truly disseminate to the masses. The '90s killed off the "truth, justice, and American way" Superman for the first time in DC's 1992 "The Death of Superman" comic. Every boy's childhood wrestling hero of the 1980s, Hulk Hogan, who taught us to "train, say your prayers, and eat your vitamins," turned heel, donned an all-black outfit, and convinced us that all of that flag-waving sincerity and traditional values stuff he preached was just an act to sell tickets and action figures.

Larry David, cocreator of the '90s greatest sitcom *Seinfeld*, famously gave the writers and cast two rules that they had to follow at all times: no hugging and no learning. Characters in this comedy, popularly dubbed "the show about nothing," should never demonstrate basic virtues of selfless love and concern for each other, and they should never learn anything from their failures.

The formula of laughing while you learn some moral lesson had been the blueprint for sitcoms going back to *I Love Lucy* and *Leave It to Beaver*. Larry David and Jerry Seinfeld felt the need to break the mold and deconstruct the genre. The series finale ended with Jerry, Elaine, George, and Kramer sentenced to prison for mocking an overweight man who was being carjacked instead of helping him, violating a local Good Samaritan law. For two consecutive episodes, nearly every supporting character from the past seasons stood on the witness stand to attest to the protagonists' utter apathy and lack of concern for anyone or anything. It seemed that nihilism had become *must-see TV*.

In film, music, TV, and real life, cynicism and a break-stuff ethos had moved into the most popular and powerful areas of our culture. And all of a sudden, we weren't just living in a story—we were in an *anti*-story.

IT WASN'T ALWAYS LIKE THIS

American culture wasn't always this cynical. The appetite for irony, subversion, and deconstruction hadn't always been so strong. If you were alive before the cynical vibe shift, you might remember how different it felt.

Imagine back to a Friday night in 1989. You and your friends have just rented a copy of *Rocky IV* on VHS from Blockbuster for the umpteenth time. Can you remember the feeling you had when Rocky was training in the snow, outrunning the KGB agents up a mountain, and overhead-pressing a wooden carriage? You weren't rolling your eyes. You weren't deconstructing the geopolitical narratives about who the real "evil empire" was during the Cold War with the Soviets. When the synth melody in John Cafferty's "Heart's on Fire" drops just as that Rocky training montage starts, you could feel your heart on fire.

If you were born after 1990, it might be impossible to imagine that people actually felt that way. That kind of earnestness fell out of fashion during the break-stuff years. If the only loss were the unironic action-movie hero, it might have been tolerable, but the change in culture touched so much more. It changed everything.

Rocky defeated Ivan Drago, the Berlin Wall fell, and we had defeated the "evil empire" of the Soviet Union. When the Cold War ended, it was like the binary good-versus-evil narrative that defined post–World War II American culture had collapsed. The political scientist Francis Fukuyama famously called it "the end of history."[2] The good guys won and the story had ended, so why weren't we living in our promised utopia?

The sense that the story previous generations had given us was a lie became pervasive. The first generation raised entirely on TV (Gen X) had come of age. They had consumed more advertisements over the course of their life than any prior generation, and they had the sneaking suspicion that those stories about good guys and bad guys, objective truth, and even religion were just one big commercial trying to sell you something. Irony and cynicism were the defense mechanisms against being sold to.

Postmodernism was now in the mainstream.

Postmodernism is a philosophical movement that questions objective truths, claims of universal values, and ultimate guiding stories, emphasizing instead the subjective, fragmented, and socially constructed nature of reality. Its inclination toward challenging authority, tradition, and any idea of a single, overarching meaning or truth began brewing in academic circles in the mid-twentieth century, but it hadn't truly hit the pop-culture zeitgeist until the 1990s.

As you'll come to better understand in chapter 5, the postmodern claim—that all overarching, guiding stories are attempts to maintain or secure power and are deserving of critique and deconstruction—acted like a sledgehammer, tearing down the values, traditions, and assumptions of the past.

It would not be a historical anomaly for the traditions of one generation to be critiqued by the next. In fact, the nineteenth-century German philosopher Georg Wilhelm Friedrich Hegel argued that this is how the zeitgeist, the "spirit of the age," shifts, but what happened in the 1990s and at the turn of the millennium was different. Mass media and the internet had no historical comparison. These innovations amplified a shift in the "spirit of the age" to a degree we still cannot fully comprehend.

The first mechanized printing press, developed by Johannes Gutenberg around 1440, enabled the mass production of books and other printed materials. The effect of this innovation produced the Renaissance, the Protestant Reformation, and the Enlightenment. Shouldn't we expect the impact of mass media and the internet to be even more profound?

And what happens when an ideology that calls you to question everything gets disseminated to the masses on a scale unlike anything the world has ever seen before?

ENSLAVING LIBERATION

The award-winning novelist David Foster Wallace was arguably the greatest author of Generation X. Wallace saw how the postmodern zeitgeist shift had been brewing for decades in hipster high culture, and in the late 1990s—as he grew exhausted with its emptiness—foretold its inevitable end. He believed that postmodernism's propensity to destroy the stories that had come before made it "patricidal" and would produce a generation that felt enslaved to cynicism. "Irony's gone from liberating to enslaving," wrote Wallace a little over ten years before he tragically took his own life.[3]

What would it mean for us to kill the stories, values, and traditions of our fathers? What would life as a story orphan feel like? Could you even navigate life without a guiding story that you believed was true?

These were the kinds of questions Wallace personally wrestled with until the very end. He instinctively understood that there was a connection between the stories we believe to be true about the world and that old religious notion of worship. In a 2005 commencement address, Wallace warned that you cannot live without a story that guides your life, and you cannot live without worshipping something:

> Because here's something else that's weird but true: In the day-to-day trenches of adult life, there is actually no such thing as atheism. There is no such thing as not worshipping. Everybody worships. The only choice we get is what to worship.
>
> And the compelling reason for maybe choosing some sort of god or spiritual-type thing to worship . . . is that pretty much anything else you worship will eat you alive.

> If you worship money and things, if they are where you tap real meaning in life, then you will never have enough, never feel you have enough. It's the truth. Worship your body and beauty and sexual allure, and you will always feel ugly. And when time and age start showing, you will die a million deaths before they finally grieve you.[4]

YOU LIVE IN A STORY

If we are to make sense of the meaning crisis and find our way out together, we must understand the power of story in shaping our souls. We must understand that sitting in a crowded movie theater, turning on the TV or Netflix, or picking up an imaginative sci-fi paperback has never been merely entertainment. Look at the online vitriol that breaks out when the Star Wars franchise makes a controversial story decision. Go to a comic con and observe the thousands of people cosplaying the archetypal heroes that most inspire them. Look at the budget for each summer's top box-office Hollywood hits.

This is not merely entertainment akin to playing a game of checkers or riding on a roller coaster. These are our guiding stories, our modern myths, and they are central to our process of finding and making meaning out of our experiences of the world.[5]

Humans are storied creatures. Unlike any other species in creation, we possess an insatiable appetite to find meaning in life. And yet we aren't born into the world with answers to why we are here and what purpose, if any, there is to our existence. So each generation, across all times and all cultures, passes on to their children what they believe is most sacred and meaningful, not by handing them spreadsheets filled with scientific data but by telling them stories.

From ancient biblical stories to modern tales of heroism that fill the pages of comic books, these guiding stories become our navigational system for finding our place in life. When we tuck our kids into bed at night and want to pass on some morsel of wisdom, we tell stories. When we honor our dead at funerals, we tell stories. When we are working through a point of pain in our lives on the therapist's couch, we tell stories.

In every decision you've ever made about a career, a spouse, or where you will live, you've imagined a possible story. How we navigate each day is shaped by the story we believe is true.

So what happens to our souls under the constant consumption of subversive, deconstructive stories? What changes in us when the stories of our formative years consistently portray the cynic as the ideal? What becomes of a people who have been told their entire lives that all guiding stories simply mask a play for power?

A fundamental disposition of cynicism forms within their souls.

For an entire generation raised in the wake of that *anti-story*, with no remembrance of a time in culture when one could sit in a theater and watch an unironically sincere *Rocky IV* without a tinge of cynical skepticism or suspicion of sincerity, irony became our native tongue. We subverted our fairy tales, killed Superman, and abandoned the religious faith of our parents and grandparents. Make no mistake: As we will see throughout this book, these are all related. To those who have lived as story orphans, ironic critique is no longer experienced as liberation but as demoralizing enslavement. Sitting now in the rubble of all that we have dismantled, many are wondering, "How did we get here? Where do we go from here?"

THE SEARCH FOR A BETTER STORY

We cannot live in a vacuum of story. It's not sustainable. As a result, something has begun to shift in American culture as we move through the 2020s. We're slowly allowing ourselves to hope that there may be a guiding story we can inhabit that affirms truth, goodness, and beauty once again. Maybe we can feel something sincere or even something *wholesome* again?

Critically acclaimed films, streaming series, and even commercials are starting to break free from the grip of cynicism and reject the libertine tendency to dissolve all our ties to tradition. What did you feel when you stepped out of the theater after watching *Top Gun: Maverick* (2022)? How did you feel watching the sincerity and earnestness of a new, brightly clad *Superman* (2025) juxtaposed against a world still stuck in the cynicism of the past?

Doesn't the aspirational and hopeful feeling you get when you watch those stories give you the sensation of catching your first breath of air after being held underwater for far too long? Maybe sincerity really is the new punk rock.

Is it too far-fetched to think that this hopeful feeling welling up might nudge you back toward church or toward being a person who shoulders a weight of moral responsibility in the community? As we will see throughout the course of this book, there are plenty of philosophical, theological, and scientific reasons to believe that this is exactly what consuming these stories does to us.

Rumbling beneath the surface of our cultural zeitgeist, this shift has already begun; the spirit of our age is changing. We finally saw enough of what that final scene of *Fight Club* warned about when The Pixies sang over the cinematic shots of chaotic destruction, "Your head will collapse, but there's nothing in it."[6]

We have felt that collapse in American culture, and we are done with living in ruin. We're ready to build something good and grow something beautiful. We want a new language beyond our cynicism. The signs of a new seismic cultural and spiritual shift toward sincerity and hope are dawning on the horizon.

To all of those dealing with the exhaustion of the soul that has accompanied our cynical age and left wondering where we go from here, allow me to show you in the following pages. For those who for most of their lives have known only declining church attendance and declining trust in our institutions, who have been swimming in the nihilism at the core of our formative pop-culture phenomena, and who have dealt with the nagging sense of despair, this journey is for you.

Together we will better understand the shifts beyond the typical culture-war jargon and partisan political tribalism, even coming to appreciate why calls to tear it all down or rage against the machine had such strong appeal. We will see that, for all the talk of subverting the system, it has been this very system of subversion that programmed our souls to despair and threatened to destroy all that was good and all that genuinely needed reform.

But we will also trace *how* the vibe has shifted and why the stakes aren't just personal—they're civilizational.

Cultural and spiritual renewal is bubbling up to the surface of American life once again. The time to rebuild is now. The "Did you ever notice?" of *Seinfeld*, directed toward making fun of the emptiness and absurdity of our mundane lives, is shifting to "Did you ever notice how meaningful it all is?" The return to meaning is here, and you have some role to play in rebuilding out of the ruins.

It might begin with the smallest step, like exchanging the protective, ironic facade you carry into conversations with even your closest friends for a moment of sincerity. Or it might look like creating the next generation of stories and scripts for Netflix that stir people's curiosity, wonder, and awe of the Transcendent. Or it may just look like you saddling up next to an aged and seasoned saint in an old pew, singing "Great Is Thy Faithfulness" shoulder to shoulder and just seeing where it goes from there.

But before we look ahead toward the possibility and promise of cultural and spiritual renewal, let's attempt to better understand how we got here by examining the power of story and why we all long to live in a true story.

CHAPTER 2

You Live in a Story, and a Story Lives in You

The destiny of the world is determined less
by the battles that are lost and won than
by the stories it loves and believes in.
Harold Clarke Goddard

My father sat on the edge of my bed as I begged for one more story before lights out. I was four years old—brimming with wonder, comforted by Dad's fables, and stalling for any excuse to stay up just a few minutes later. Without a book in hand, he began a classic tale: "Once upon a time . . ."

My favorite beat in this particular story was when the villain of the story arrived on the scene and announced, "I'll huff, and I'll puff, and I'll __________."

If English is your native tongue, you likely filled in that blank with ease. The moment you read the first few words, it may have even felt like the remaining phrase, "blow your house down," simply emerged from your subconscious without you having to actively search through file folders in your brain to recall the words.

Of course this phrase comes from the story "The Three Little Pigs" and is part of the infamous threat that the big bad wolf howls at each little pig before attempting to destroy their homes with a gust of wind from his seemingly superpowered lung capacity. But how do you know this story? And maybe the better question is—*why* do you know this story?

Though numerous iterations of "The Three Little Pigs" exist in children's books and animated media, my earliest memory of this tale doesn't come from any book or movie. It comes from the still-vivid recollections of my dad reciting it before bed as a young child, replete with humorous voices for the big bad wolf and the pigs.

When he told me of the menacing wolf and described the materials the three pigs chose to build their homes with, my dad wasn't reading the story from a book. He didn't have notes written on his arm like some inexperienced professional wrestler about to cut an awkwardly braggadocious promo backstage. He didn't need a script, just some wildly inconsistent pig voices, a threatening growl that sounded like a close cousin to his Cookie Monster impersonation, and a captive audience that would do anything to stay up even a little past bedtime.

This was a story my dad knew from memory because it was a bedtime story that his parents had told him, and my grandparents had heard it from their parents before that. How far back does the transmission of "The Three Little Pigs" go?

Folklore and fairy-tale scholars are confident that long before this story was first published in 1843, people had passed on this fable in a way not all that different from how my father passed it on to me—through word-of-mouth storytelling. The oral tradition of "The Three Little Pigs" likely dates back to the 1600s.

The better question remains, *Why* do we know this strange story at all? Why has this story about talking pigs been circulating throughout the English-speaking world for over four hundred years? If you pause to think about the details, they don't make much sense. Pigs building houses? A wolf just blowing them down? It's obviously absurd. But if you think back to when you were young, the real-world absurdity of these details didn't matter to you. Talking animals exist in all sorts of children's movies and shows, and I've never heard a young child complain, "This is so unrealistic. Turn it off!" Even from an early age, we intrinsically understand that "The Three Little Pigs" has something deeper it's trying to convey through symbolism.

STORIED CREATURES AND OUR QUEST FOR MEANING

"The Three Little Pigs" is an example of a guiding story—one that a culture produces and preserves to transmit values to its people and to help them understand what that culture has concluded about the meaning of life. Another way of putting it is that these guiding stories are intended to pass on a life strategy and help people navigate what should be of ultimate concern in their lives.

With "The Three Little Pigs" and other bedtime stories, children are often asked afterward to reflect on the moral of the story. In this case, the moral centers around this basic idea: Hard work pays off in the long run, while laziness and taking shortcuts leads to ruin. That's a life strategy.

This story has lived on for over four hundred years because our shared culture, and the cultures it descended from, wanted to transmit values to their children that they enshrined as central to a successful life strategy: If you want a successful life, one that is best prepared for the potential of sudden catastrophe or the ups and downs of daily living, you'd better work hard now and sacrifice some of your present comforts. By doing that, you can secure a more stable future that minimizes your likelihood of suffering.

That is a profound piece of wisdom to try to digest at four years old, but this is the magic of narrative. By imagining ourselves inside a story, we can internalize these complex values from even the earliest ages.

It's not just fables at bedtime either. You were given countless guiding stories throughout your childhood. Whether it was Bible stories you might have heard at Sunday school or a favorite movie your family watched during family movie night, these stories were passed on to give you a life strategy and to help you answer some of the most essential questions of meaning: Why am I here? What's the point of life? What does the good life look like?

There's a reason why parents don't give their kids a lecture with a PowerPoint presentation before bed or hand them a spreadsheet filled with data and statistics when they want to transmit their values. Lectures and spreadsheets have their place, but when it comes to communicating values and the meaning of life, they simply can't compare to a good story.

This is because humans are storied creatures. We instinctively interpret our lives and the world through stories. This ability to create and understand stories comes from a more fundamental ability to recognize patterns. The human brain is a pattern-seeking organ. Like many species on this planet, we rely on pattern-detection skills for survival. If you can't pick up on the patterns of what can kill you, life is going to be a pretty short ride.

Humans are the only species in all of creation that take patterns and turn them into stories, though. Your dog isn't doing that after scarfing down a bowl of Kibbles 'n Bits. The gazelle isn't writing a memoir after escaping a pride of lions. Storytelling is a higher-order function of our brains that draws on our ability to recognize patterns and link them together in a purposeful sequence. That sequence helps us remember relevant patterns more easily through a process called *memory encoding*. Studies show that learning from a "well-told story is remembered more accurately and for much longer than information learned from facts and figures."[1] Amazingly, we are twenty times more likely to remember crucial facts if they are part of a story.[2]

But it's not just that storytelling is an adaptive survival trait. You could memorize an entire library of stories replete with competent survival strategies and still feel an absence of meaning in your life. As cognitive scientist and philosopher John Vervaeke argues, the need for meaning is so strong that a person can override their survival instinct and tragically choose to end their own life if they don't see themselves in a meaningful story.[3]

NARRATIVE IDENTITY AND OUR QUEST FOR A TRUE STORY

Once, when I was probably seven or eight years old, my parents temporarily banned *Teenage Mutant Ninja Turtles* from our home because someone at church said Master Splinter was teaching Eastern religions. That was a top-five most devastating day of my childhood. So I respectfully threw a challenge flag, and upon further review by my parents, the call was overturned. My parents concluded that while the teachings of Master Splinter were occasionally dressed up as mystical insights from the Orient, it was basically the same generic advice Yoda or Mr. Miyagi from *The Karate Kid* was doling out and probably wasn't going to cause me to convert to Shintoism. Thankfully, Turtle Time was back in the Anleitner house.

In hindsight I understand why my parents were concerned. No animated anthropomorphic rat dressed in a gi was going to undo the values that they were working so hard to instill in their child. Though none of us would have used these exact terms at the time, my parents were concerned about how a potentially different guiding story from the one they wanted to instill in me might be nestled within that Saturday-morning cartoon, affecting my *narrative identity*, and forever changing the course of my life.

That might sound overly dramatic, but it really isn't. Entire civilizations will take drastic measures to keep out certain kinds of stories that they suspect might act like a Trojan horse to undermine the story and values they want instilled in their people. For example, in 2011 the Chinese government issued guidelines effectively banning time-travel stories from prime-time television. Their fear was that time-travel stories suggest history is malleable or could have gone differently—a dangerous notion for a regime seeking to curtail the potentially revolutionary belief that a single individual could change history. Tough luck for all the Chinese sci-fi lovers out there pulling for a prime-time *Timecop* spin-off to get made, but their government clearly gets the power of story to change someone's narrative identity.

What do I mean by *narrative identity*? Imagine the last time you met a new neighbor or coworker and they said, "So tell me about yourself." You didn't robotically list a bunch of random facts: "I'm six feet tall. I have brown hair. I'm allergic to cats." Instead, you shared some of the running autobiography that you keep in your head.

This story you told is part of your narrative identity. This term—coined by psychologist Dan McAdams—is your internalized life story. It is how you integrate your past (where you come from), your present (who you believe you are now), and your future aspirations (who you want to be) into a meaningful pattern and a unified sense of self.[4] This internal story is shaped by the guiding stories of your surrounding culture and your experiences of the world. (Note: There are conditions such as Alzheimer's, autism spectrum disorder, or traumatic brain injury that can prevent narrative identity from forming.)

So what stories have most shaped your story? Where did they come from? If you've never asked yourself these questions, now is as good a time as any. Because those stories given to you—whether by your parents, your school, or Hollywood—not only shape your own personal story but become the lens through which you interpret the world. As the sociologist Christian Smith writes, humans are "animals who make stories but also animals who are *made* by our stories."[5]

Is the world really this dark, meaningless place where only the most cynical among us can avoid being mercilessly enslaved by the system? That depends. Which story has *made* you? Remember, the story you're living in is also a lens through which you interpret the world. So is your story based on a true story?

One of the best examples of this comes from sociologist George Gerbner, who performed a groundbreaking study on mean world syndrome in the late 1960s. Gerbner's research demonstrated that people who continually consumed violent or dystopian media tended to develop a more fearful, pessimistic view of reality. In other words, by consuming stories that communicate that the world is terrible, you begin to overestimate how terrible the world actually is.[6]

I don't have a dog (despite my children's adamant pleading), but I hear from dog owners that if you feed it, give it plenty of attention, and take it for walks, a dog is fairly content. Dogs don't have a narrative identity. They aren't wrestling with existential questions about why they are here or what the point of life is. It is not in their nature as dogs. But this quest for meaning is in our nature, and it is such an essential drive in the human condition that a human being can have food, shelter, and even sit in lavish material comfort and still feel a profound emptiness in their soul.

The theologian Stanley Grenz argued that this is one of the key differences between humans and every animal on the planet. We are constantly questioning, struggling, and even reshaping our environments "in an unfulfilled attempt to create a 'home' for ourselves."[7] This home we seek is the deep sense within our souls that we have found and fulfilled our purpose in life.

THE SCIENTIFIC NEED TO LIVE IN A MEANINGFUL STORY

At some point in your life—it could be at a funeral for a friend, or when the 2 a.m. epiphany hits that you've been doomscrolling on your phone in bed for the last three hours, or just on a random Tuesday afternoon when you're deep into hour seven of macrodata refinement at the office—you've probably had the thought: "What exactly is the point of all this?"

Maybe someone has literally talked you off a ledge before, but this might just feel like a low-grade existential ache, like all the pieces in your story aren't connecting together and fitting squarely with reality. Most of the time this ache is just a bit of white noise that you can drown out with a healthy dose of motivational David Goggins clips on YouTube, but occasionally it comes screaming through the void and demands your attention.

It's best not to keep stuffing that question back into some dark closet in your mind, because this isn't a bug of the human experience. It's a feature. You and I need meaning.

So what exactly are we looking for? In the scientific literature on the psychology of meaning, a helpful framework has emerged for addressing this question. There are three pillars that support our sense of meaning in life: coherence, purpose, and significance.[8] If the guiding story we situate our own story within cannot address these core needs, we will feel a nagging absence of meaning.

Coherence is about whether we can pick up on any repeatable pattern in the world. It is the sense that we can understand the world and that reality runs on some predictable order instead of being random and chaotic. Take the opening lines of the Teacher found in the biblical book of Ecclesiastes, which sound as if they could have been uttered by Friedrich Nietzsche or Kurt Cobain: "Meaningless! Meaningless! . . . Utterly meaningless! Everything is meaningless" (Ecclesiastes 1:2). The Teacher of Ecclesiastes searches the world for any repeating, discernible pattern, any rhyme or reason as to why things are the way they are. The Teacher is looking for *coherence.* Without a sense of coherence, life doesn't make sense. The less coherent the world feels, the more confused, depressed, or apathetic we become.

The second pillar that supports our sense of meaning in life is *purpose.* If we can detect a coherent pattern in the world, what is that pattern pointing to as the ultimate goal? Purpose seeks to answer the question of whether there is an overarching goal in life. Where is this story headed?

The renowned biologist Richard Dawkins, who was heralded as one of the "Four Horsemen of New Atheism" in the mid-2000s, once wrote, "The universe that we observe has precisely the properties we should expect if there is, at bottom, no design, no purpose, no evil, no good, nothing but pitiless indifference."[9] Dawkins sees *coherence* but not *purpose.* Later in this book, we'll see why a wave of former Dawkins disciples have ditched this philosophy—though you can probably piece together for yourself why a story without a point might eventually lose a few followers.

If we are to find a sustaining sense of meaning in life, we will need to find a guiding story that has a clear sense of coherence and points us to an ultimate goal—or *telos*—in life. For the ancient Greek philosopher Aristotle, understanding a thing's telos or its final goal was the central question in determining its meaning and purpose. Figuring out the material stuff that made up a particular thing was important, like how a piece of wood made up the material of a dining room table, but simply being able to identify what made a thing (its material cause) doesn't automatically explain *why* it was made and what purpose it was made for. The meaning of a wooden table is not determined by naming what it is made from but by naming its maker's purpose in creating it. When a family sits at their dining room table for dinner, sharing a meal and a loving connection, that table fulfills its telos.

We all long to know our telos. For a guiding story to fulfill our longing for meaning, it must be able to tell us what the story is all about. It must give us a direction to aim for. If we cannot find an overarching goal in life, we will not be able to figure out what role, if any, we are to play in that purpose. We will be aimless.

This brings us to the third pillar that supports a sense of meaning in life: *significance*. Significance is about answering the questions, "What role do I play in the overarching purpose of life? Do I matter to the world and others?" You might believe that the world is filled with a coherent structure and may even see some cosmic purpose to it all, but if you struggle to see what role *you* play in it, you'll still feel an absence of meaning.

How does *my* life matter in this story? What value does my life have to others?

This is why stories that show us a hero's journey—a pattern of storytelling that twentieth-century expert in comparative mythology Joseph Campbell called the "monomyth"—so deeply resonate with us. In the common hero's journey, which we find in everything from Homer's *The Odyssey* to J. R. R. Tolkien's *The Lord of the Rings* and George Lucas's *Star Wars*, we see a person embark on a purposeful quest that pushes them beyond the bounds of their comforts and toward a destination that transforms them into a person of significance.

These stories resonate with us because in them we see how a character moves from a state of seeming insignificance to becoming a person with a significant role to play in the overarching purpose of that story. Significance does not mean that we all must save the galaxy like Luke Skywalker, but it does mean that we should feel like we are playing some unique role in a bigger story that matters to others.

Of these three pillars—coherence, purpose, and significance—do any feel shaky in your life right now? When you feel that existential ache, is it because the story feels random, because you can't see where it's supposed to go, or because you aren't sure you're playing a unique role in a bigger story at all? Remember, you can try to drown out these questions or numb the palpable dissonance, but these are coping strategies that only put despair on temporary layaway. You are a storied creature with an innate longing for meaning, which cannot be supported without a sense that the story you're in is coherent and purposeful, and gives you a significant role that matters to others.

SPIRITUAL YEARNINGS FOR A STORY THAT HOLDS IT ALL TOGETHER

Among many of those scientists of the mind, the consensus has begun to shift away from a picture of human beings as mechanical meat suits who've evolved beyond the need for anything that whiffs of the primitive religious impulses found in our ancient ancestors. For reasons we'll explore in chapter 3, many of us were led to believe that our yearnings for the spiritual, for a taste of the Transcendent, are just for fourth-century desert mystics or people who live in Southeast Portland. They're not.

That view was part of a reality-distorting story in our culture that has always been foreign to anyone not living in the West over the past few hundred years. The religious impulse doesn't have an off switch.

You'll find this longing in people of every culture, because it is baked into human nature. It is the quest to find the *ultimate* guiding story—the ultimate true story that all other true stories derive their trueness from.

Even though we've seen the church pews empty out over the past several decades, spiritual yearnings haven't disappeared in our culture. Over 70 percent of those who claim to be "spiritual but not religious" believe they've experienced spiritual energies in trees, crystals, and other parts of nature.[10] Thirty percent of American adults consult astrology, tarot, or psychic services at least once a year—roughly the same percentage as those who go to church regularly.[11] A 2024 study published in *The International Journal for the Psychology of Religion* confirmed that nones don't necessarily have fewer spiritual yearnings than those who identify as religious; they just "do so in myriad ways, yet they may prefer personalized means of discovery to those offered by traditional religions."[12]

For all of you reading this anywhere in Western civilization, whether you grew up a Christian or a Buddhist or a none, whether you hail from a ranch in West Texas or were born and raised in South Detroit (which is something no one from Detroit has ever said unless they were singing along), we've all been shaped by powerful, culture-wide guiding stories. These have run like a default philosophical operating system in the background of our civilization.

How have these guiding stories shaped your story? The first step toward answering that question begins by understanding those stories, where they came from, and how they show up in the arenas of culture that influence us all. If the cognitive scientists are right and we are hardwired for coherence, purpose, and significance, then the crisis we felt in the late '90s wasn't just a Limp Bizkit–induced bad mood—it was a structural failure of the story we were living in. To understand why we ended up with a sledgehammer in our hands, standing amid the rubble of deconstruction, we will need to understand where these guiding stories came from and what they mean.

Throughout the last five hundred years, Western culture has been shaped by three distinct guiding stories: the Traditional Story, which anchored us in a fixed, divinely ordered cosmos; the Modern Story, which handed us the pen and told us to write our own destiny through reason, progress, and epic training montage scenes; and the Postmodern Anti-Story, which urged us to *see through* those two stories—and every other story—as mere power plays.[13] You and I are walking around today with fragments of all three stuck in our narrative identities, and we're trying to figure out if the best of each could somehow be synthesized together or if they point to some kind of meta-guiding story, a *story of stories.*

To make sense of the mess and figure out where we go from here, we need to do a little forensic accounting. We need to trace the breadcrumbs back to where the most formative stories of our generation began and then go back to the future. Unless you're reading this in China, where that kind of Doc Brown–inspired time travel is frowned upon.

We need to see how we moved from a world where the word *religion* didn't really exist but was still everywhere to a world of machine-like rationality where religion became a private enterprise only to end up in a show about nothing. To do that we have to leave the present day and head back to a time when a different kind of rebel decided it was time to challenge the story he was raised in.

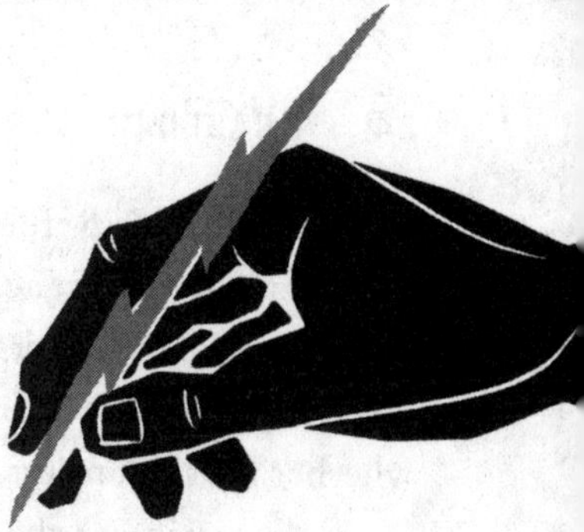

CHAPTER 3

The Modern Story

Man is nothing else but what he makes of himself.
Jean-Paul Sartre

He was a rule breaker. A rebel with a cause. The old guard in charge disliked him. He spoke boldly, pushed boundaries, and refused to fall in line. You've seen his maverick type before. His type is the kind you'd find in the cockpit of a fighter jet, cracking wise as he sophomorically buzzes the tower.

But this isn't *Top Gun*. It's Wittenberg, 1517, and without Martin Luther you probably wouldn't think of Tom Cruise's Maverick as a hero, or cheer for a whip-wielding archaeologist named Indiana Jones, or see the defiant nonconformity of Steve Jobs as an admirable mark of brilliance.

If you're a Boomer, Gen Xer, or elder Millennial, the reason why you might see these figures as heroic is because you were born into an America shaped by a unique guiding story—one that would never have existed without Martin Luther.

On October 31, 1517, a seemingly insignificant German priest posted a list of ninety-five grievances with the Roman Catholic Church. This simple act was the spark that ignited a religious revolution known as the Protestant Reformation. Luther's radical claim was that every individual had direct access to God through faith in Jesus Christ without the need for priests, bishops, or popes to function as mediators. Christ was the sole mediator of grace and truth, and every person—whether peasant, priest, or king—could individually access the source of truth, bypassing the institutional authority of the Church, which had claimed to function as the divinely designated mediator between God and humanity.

This idea germinated in unforeseen ways, eventually reshaping the entire guiding story of the West through the Scientific Revolution and the Enlightenment and giving birth to the Modern Story. Before the Modern Story, the Western mind had been shaped throughout the Medieval period by the Traditional Story. In the Traditional Story your place in life was divinely ordained. If you were born as a peasant, your goal in life was to be a peasant who was faithful to the God-ordained duties of all peasants. If you were born a king, your throne was established by God, and your moral responsibility was to rightly govern over the institutions that held and maintained the providentially ordained social order. These institutions of the Church and crown were the arbiters and mediators of the truth to the masses.

Try imagining the serf in AD 1230 sitting on a haystack having an existential crisis about whether he's "living his truth." That wasn't a thing in those days. Sure, they were fully formed people with the faculties and desires all of us share, but their worldview was profoundly different, and that deeply affected every aspect of their lives. For the premodern mind shaped by the Traditional Story, truth wasn't something you found inside yourself. It was handed down from the top—Church, crown, God. You simply didn't question it.

But what if you came to believe that, regardless of your status on the social ladder, you as an individual had access to God? That you could weigh the claims of Scripture for yourself? And what if the Word of God could suddenly be read in *your* native tongue, as Luther made available in German and William Tyndale translated into English? If you have access to God in the same way that your priest or king does, then maybe they aren't above you. Maybe *you* are their equal.

If that is the case, then you aren't defying God's will by defying the pope or a king. You may even be doing God's will. If one meager German priest could change the world, then what might any courageous individual who defiantly pursues the truth be able to accomplish?

Just over a century after Luther posted his Ninety-Five Theses, the philosopher René Descartes wrote, "I think, therefore I am." Descartes took Luther's belief that the individual can directly access the truth in Christ to an entirely different level: It wasn't just the Church you could bypass but literally everything—until it could be proven with absolute rational certainty.

According to Descartes, the starting point for truth itself was the mind of the individual. He argued that all beliefs should be questioned until they could be proven rationally, and he categorically split the spiritual and the material into separate boxes so that the material world could be rationally studied like the workings of a machine.[1] The mind of the average person living in the Traditional Story did not separate the spiritual and material. Rain fell, crops grew, angels helped, demons meddled, and all of it meant something. It's only after Descartes and the Enlightenment (1685–1815) put it through the metaphysical paper shredder that people started believing the spiritual was separate from their physical reality. And to this day most Western minds still struggle to reintegrate those realities.

Cartesian ideas influenced scientific revolutionaries like Isaac Newton, who came to believe that if the universe functioned like a machine, then even the planets weren't moved by God but by automatic, natural forces. These ideas changed our entire way of seeing the world and our place in it. They changed our guiding story.

The Scientific Revolution (1543–1687) and the Enlightenment (1685–1815) killed the Traditional Story and eventually gave birth to a new Modern Story. Instead of believing that your place in life was determined by cosmic forces, your status in life was now up to you. Church authorities, kings, and governments did not deserve unquestioned subservience. Remember, you had the same access and standing with God. You could even challenge the leaders. You could bring about revolutionary changes like the American and French Revolutions, which were deeply shaped by the Modern Story.

In the revolutionary manifesto that declared American independence from the British crown, Thomas Jefferson argued that it was the individual's divine right to overthrow unjust authorities. In this new guiding story, if someone stands in the way of truth, you not only have permission but a moral responsibility to defy them and charge onward toward the truth. Because of this, the worth of a person wasn't determined by the position or status they were born into, but by what they made of their life.

The Modern Story was essential to the development of the American identity. There is no United States of America without this guiding story. Because of its central role in our culture's foundational myth as a nation conceived in liberty, the values of the Modern Story have historically been treated as the sacred values of American culture. As we'll see in the next chapter, some of these sacred values of the Modern Story began to be challenged in the 1960s, which inevitably led to a culture war over competing guiding stories. But you won't be able to understand that ideological struggle, nor will you be able to understand how these values have shaped your own story, without being able to identify the core values of the Modern Story.

Think back to the moment you first moved out on your own. Maybe you were eighteen, packing up a beat-up sedan with everything you owned to head off to college, or you were twentysomething and standing in an empty apartment with nothing but a mattress, a job you just started in a brand-new town, and a heart full of dreams. Remember that flutter in your chest? That was more than just nerves. It was the intoxicating belief that your life was your own to write. And the deep-seated belief that your choices matter, you aren't just a pawn of fate, and you have the agency to build a future better than the one you were handed? That hasn't always been something people believed about their own story. The medieval peasant didn't see themselves living in a story like this, but you do. That is the impact of the Modern Story.

From its conception the Modern Story has placed one value above nearly all others: *individualism*. It celebrates the power of the self. Individuals, not groups or institutions, are celebrated as the center of the story. In the Modern Story we celebrate fearless adventurers like Christopher Columbus, self-made entrepreneurs like Benjamin Franklin and Henry Ford, and brash, rebellious heroes like *Top Gun*'s Maverick and Indiana Jones.

These men are lauded as heroes within this guiding story because of another essential value of the Modern Story: *meritocracy*, which is the belief that one's place in life is not determined by birth, class, or divine decree but by hard work, ingenuity, ambition, and moral character. In a meritocracy, competency is king.

Climb to the top of the steps just outside the Philadelphia Museum of Art, and you will see a statue of a man with arms raised high above his head, posing victorious after battle. Is it the statue of some ancient Roman deity? Is it the pose of some great American general? No. It's a statue of a fictional character from a movie franchise about boxing: Rocky Balboa.

Why would we enshrine a fictional boxer in the public square like this? Because Rocky is the quintessential, archetypal icon of the Modern Story's value of meritocracy. In *Rocky*, Sylvester Stallone's character, Rocky Balboa, was a poor, no-name boxer who hadn't been born with the greatest talent but possessed heart, work ethic, and determination.

If you've spent your whole life in American culture, you might have just assumed that stories like *Rocky* have always been around, but they haven't. Rocky is a unique creation of the values of the Modern Story, and you'd be hard-pressed to find heroes like him in Western culture during the previous reign of the Traditional Story. King Arthur became king because of divine destiny, not because he worked his way to the top. In Greek mythology, Achilles is already endowed with the strength of the gods at birth. Beowulf doesn't have any inspirational training montage scenes where he earns his muscle through a steady regimen of doing push-ups and running up flights of stairs. Long before America's first African American president, a Black family starred in the most-watched show in America for five straight seasons. *The Cosby Show* was the biggest sitcom hit of the 1980s. Setting aside the titular character's later legal troubles for a moment, how did Bill Cosby become America's father figure at a time when many still felt it would be impossible for the US to have a Black president? It's because *The Cosby Show* deeply celebrated the Modern Story and, in doing so, celebrated the core values of American culture.

The characters Bill and Clair Huxtable climbed their way into elite status in American society as a respectable doctor and lawyer through hard work and education, not because they were born into that status. In nearly every episode, you'll find Bill lecturing his son, Theo, about the value of education and pushing his children to get out of the house, get a job, and make something of their own lives. The Huxtables are all about meritocracy.

By the end of every episode, there's always some clear moral lesson the audience is supposed to learn that is presented as objectively true and universally accepted. There's not a tinge of irony or cynicism in the show. For those of us shaped by later forces of highly ironic and cynical postmodern comedies like *Rick and Morty* or *Curb Your Enthusiasm*, where any sense of objective morality is ridiculed into oblivion, watching *The Cosby Show* today might feel preachy and cringe. But that was true of most sitcoms until *Seinfeld* broke that mold (more on that later).

Some of the moral lessons may have shifted between *Leave It to Beaver* in the 1950s and *The Cosby Show* in the 1980s—after all, progress is another core value of the Modern Story—but what didn't change was the belief that objective moral truths existed and that the whole audience should agree on them. That commitment to objectivity is itself a defining value of the Modern Story.

Shaped by Enlightenment thinkers like John Locke and Immanuel Kant, who argued that humans possess both inherent rights granted by

God and nature as well as moral duties that are neither socially constructed nor relative, the Modern Story taught that right and wrong are universal and apply to all people capable of reason. Written laws, constitutions, and bills of rights are rooted in the belief that there is an objective moral standard that even rulers and kings must answer to. We can deduce moral truths just as we can deduce objective scientific truths like Newton's law of gravitation. It is this deep belief in objectivity that produces one of the most distinct flavors of the Modern Story: *sincerity*.

Go back and watch the original *Top Gun*. No self-aware and self-effacing humor or cynicism in sight. That beach volleyball scene wasn't an ironic gag. Your uncle who drove an '84 Trans Am watched that sweaty, sandy montage and went, "Heck, yeah. This is so inspirational, man," with a completely straight face. The good guys and bad guys are objectively clear, with no ethical grayness to be found in the story whatsoever. It's quintessential modern storytelling.

That clear sense of moral black and white is a big part of what made the original *Star Wars* such a huge success. When Luke Skywalker blows up the Death Star, the filmmakers aren't challenging you to consider whether it was ethical for Luke to kill all those people. I mean, he probably torpedoed a bunch of random minimum-wage workers who took jobs like washing dishes in the Death Star kitchen to pay for their kids' braces and Life Day presents. It's easier to be sincere when you believe you're objectively right.

Like Han Solo said in *Star Wars*: *A New Hope*, "Hokey religions and ancient weapons are no match for a good blaster at your side,"[2] the Modern Story placed religion in a separate box, labeled it "imaginary," and relegated it to being a private, personal matter. In the premodern world, religion wasn't a separate category for private practice, magic wasn't make-believe, and "Do you believe in God?" wasn't really a question on the table.

But the Modern Story changed all of that. Reason became the domain of public truths that we can verify and share together. Religion was downgraded to a subjective, private lifestyle choice.

In the Traditional Story theology was queen of the sciences. In the Modern Story theology is an obscure section in the back of Barnes & Noble next to the books about crystals and painfully drab analytic philosophy. As the great Esqueleto once said to his luchador wrestling partner Nacho in the Anleitner household favorite *Nacho Libre*, "I don't believe in God. I believe in science."[3] In the Modern Story science became the highest-ranking discipline for investigating reality because science was seen as disclosing objective truth.

While Luther said that you don't need a priest to know God, the Modern Story tells us that we don't need a priest or pastor to know much of anything at all. When it comes to the role of the pastor in the Modern Story, theologian Andrew Root might have summarized it best when he wrote, "The pastor can feel like an odd person, living an embarrassingly outdated vocation. At its worst, it can feel like being a full-time employee of the Renaissance Festival, playing a part from the old world that people at times appreciate (e.g., Christmas and Easter) but most often find unnecessary."[4]

For the most part, people living in the Modern Story have not been hostile to traditional religion; they just find it a bit unnecessary. It's like how you might feel about your appendix—it's fine that it's there; you just don't want it to act up and kill you.

All of our US presidents have professed to be Christian, so again, it's not that the Modern Story demonizes going to church or praying. We might even respect the private faith of a favored politician or famous athlete being occasionally professed in public. But the Modern Story has completely changed the way we categorize our experiences of the world and splits our experiences into two categories—sacred and secular.

Going to church, praying, reading the Bible, or attending a funeral are all part of this private sphere of personal, subjective meaning that we dub sacred. If you do that stuff—well, good for you, Flanders. Math, science, politics, technology, medicine, music, working a job, or watching a movie are all secular activities. That's the stuff that really matters. In the Modern Story most of your life is spent in the secular category. This has led many to describe the feeling of living in the Modern Story as a pervasive sense of *disenchantment*.

We tried to eliminate the superstitions and thus cut down on the number of women being thrown into lakes to test if they were witches or not. I'm confident we can safely call that an upgrade. We found that dealing with germs might make people healthier than spooky rituals meant to drive out evil spirits. This might decrease my favorability with the medieval crunchy mom demographic, but sign me up for some antibiotics if I come down with strep throat and leave the village shaman's magical (but 100 percent organic!) potions at home.

Reason and science seemed to be making our lives materially better in a variety of ways. That pattern-detection thing our brain is always trying to do? Science seemed like a pretty reliable tool for consistently picking up on true patterns and dispelling false ones. Maybe ol' Nacho's tag-team partner was right to just believe in science?

But people living in the Modern Story have also felt a nagging sense of incompleteness. They have wondered whether they are just cogs in a giant, soulless machine. Their jobs don't feel like sacred callings. They sell paper at a midsized paper-supply company in Scranton, Pennsylvania, so they can afford a 2004 Chrysler Sebring and a flat-screen TV. Where's the magic? Where's the sense of transcendence? Where's the meaning?

This is why the twentieth-century theologian Paul Tillich tried to help people living in the Modern Story realize that religion isn't a separate, private category at all. Religion is about that *which is of ultimate concern*. The Modern Story wasn't devoid of claims as to what should be of ultimate concern. It just redirected our ultimate concerns and highest values in a different direction from the Traditional Story.

We look at how the ancient Greeks built an idol to the goddess Athena in the Parthenon as the personification of wisdom and think, "How primitive and superstitious." But we will gladly venerate the statue of a tongue-wagging, baggy-shorts-wearing basketball demigod in Michael Jordan, whose mythic story of being cut from his varsity team in high school only to become the self-made greatest hooper of all time personifies our values of rugged individualism and meritocracy. Hanging a religious icon in your home is a private, spiritual matter, but our public schools can adorn their hallways with huge murals of Ruth Bader Ginsburg or Martin Luther King Jr. as secular saints.

If you're a pro football player, you can say a private prayer to yourself before a big playoff game, but when it is time to sing the national anthem, you'd better rise, reverently face the American flag, and even put your hand over your heart. If someone performed similar gestures in church—such as rising for the reading of Scripture, expressing reverence while singing a hymn, or lifting a hand in prayer while facing the cross—they'd be seen as expressions of worship. Why would we consider the gestures that happen at that football game to be anything less than expressions of what people believe is worthy of our love and attention—worthy of worship? Maybe we really aren't any less religious; it's just that our religions in the Modern Story are shallower.

As we learned in the previous chapter, our sense of meaning in life rests on three pillars. How did the Modern Story attempt to satisfy our longings for coherence, purpose, and significance, and did it succeed?

The Modern Story attempted to offer us a coherent story within a universe that was ordered, rational, and governed by discernible laws. From Newton's laws of motion to the structure of DNA, reality was believed to have a predictable, universal pattern that we can know objectively. The world doesn't run on chaos; it runs on reason. So to the question of, "Is there a discernible, repeatable pattern to reality that we can make sense of?" the Modern Story would answer with a resounding yes. But how does it handle the question of purpose? Is there an overarching goal to life that this coherent pattern is pointing to?

Because competency is king in the Modern Story, the purpose of life is progress. The Modern Story took Christian notions of a future, final setting right of the world, pulled out the theological core of that forward-looking impulse, put it into a private spiritual box, and declared that reason and human ingenuity alone could get us to a utopian promised land. In the Modern Story we were taught that the time before modernity was the Dark Ages, and we were told that we "were on the wrong side of history" if we didn't progress fast enough.

But unlike historic Christian visions of a union of heaven and earth, in which what is true, good, and beautiful is defined by an external source in Christ, the Modern Story's emphasis on radical individualism and self-authoring our own stories leaves us with a problem in finding the purpose of life. How does one rationally deduce what that utopian future should look like? Should it look like Adolf Hitler's vision, where we eliminate the weak, the sick, and those we deem as having inferior genetics so that we can breed a "better" race of humans? Whose notion of progress gets to decide what the goal of this story should be? Is it all decided by who has the power, as the nineteenth-century German philosopher Friedrich Nietzsche proposed?

In the Modern Story our sense of significance came from the belief that we were the authors of our own stories. You and I could make a difference. We had the ability to self-author our destiny. We replaced our ancient ancestors' proclivity to look to the stars to direct their future with looking to Hollywood stars who we could model our lives after. Much of our sense of significance rested on our ability to become a star too.

If Oprah Winfrey can rise from poverty in rural Mississippi to become a global media mogul worth $3 billion, then why can't you and I do the same? If a working-class white kid from the trailer parks of 8 Mile in Detroit—armed with just a pencil, a scratchpad, and a sweater covered in his mom's spaghetti—can become the best-selling rapper of all time, what's stopping you from becoming a star like Eminem? In the Modern Story the rags-to-riches arc is one of the primary ways we feel significant.

And don't get me wrong—maybe it's the Detroit kid in me—but I prefer living in a system where you might be able to rap your way out of your trailer park if you don't like living there. I was never in Oprah's target audience, but good for her. It wasn't all that long ago that someone who shared her skin color would have been treated as subhuman property. Her rags-to-riches story is absolutely remarkable. And yet all of our rational, scientific inquiries into what makes us happy show that emotional well-being plateaus or has very minor increases beyond middle-income levels.[5] In fact, if the pursuit of continual material progress replaces close, meaningful relationships, emotional well-being actually declines. Perpetual progress in accumulating material possessions and status at Oprah levels does not satisfy our longing for meaning in life.

The Modern Story gave us skyscrapers, constitutions, and action heroes. It taught us to chase truth with our minds, success with gritty workout montages, and meaning with our own two hands. But as empowering as that may feel, after centuries of living in that story, many began to sense that something vital was missing. Sure, the Modern Story felt coherent. The rational universe was a closed system of cause and effect. We could master it with tools and technology, but for what end? We learned how to build rockets but forgot how to feel wonder. We no longer lived in a sacred cosmic drama. We lived in a machine.

History was headed somewhere, and we could make it a better world across many material metrics. We cured diseases and increased human life expectancy beyond anything we've seen since the dawn of human history. But the same scientific rationality that built hospitals also built gas chambers at Auschwitz. Our technological progress did not automatically equate to moral progress. And what is all this progress for? More productivity? More profit? Like, why exactly are we going to Mars, Elon?

The Modern Story told us that we are significant because we are individuals who can rise above our circumstances and forge our own destinies. It gave individuals a sense of dignity and autonomy that had not been present in the Traditional Story. But building a sense of significance on your ability to self-author your life also comes with the costly side effect of living in a steady state of low-grade existential anxiety. "What if what I'm doing isn't enough? What if I achieve, achieve, and achieve some more and still feel like I haven't arrived?"

David Byrne of the new-wave band Talking Heads perfectly captured the feeling of our perpetual production and low-grade existential anxiety in the 1980 song "Once in a Lifetime." He portrays a successful modern man who suddenly "wakes up" in a beautiful house with a beautiful wife and realizes he has no idea *why* he arrived at this superficially pleasant yet unfulfilling destination. He questions the trajectory of his life—asking himself if he is right or wrong about it all—before spiraling into the dreadful realization of the vanity of his pursuits. "Same as it ever was . . . same as it ever was," he repeatedly drones. Eventually, his self-authored identity cracks in existential terror: "My God, what have I done?"[6]

In the next chapter we'll look at the moment when the Modern Story began to crack—when its confident objectivity gave way to cynical critique, its sincerity gave way to irony, and its claim to be the universally true story gave way to the suspicion that no guiding story could ever be trusted again.

Enter the Postmodern Anti-Story.

CHAPTER 4

The Postmodern Anti-Story

Facts do not exist, only interpretations.
Friedrich Nietzsche

"Well, what's the show about?" Jerry asks as he sends George a puzzled look across the small diner table.

"It's about nothing," George replies.

Jerry, still perplexed, retorts, "No story?"

"No! Forget the story," George quips back with a confident smile. "Everybody's doing something; we'll do nothing."

Jerry's eyes begin to squint as he mulls over George's proposal. "So, we go into NBC, and we tell them we've got an idea for a show about nothing?"

"Exactly!"

"They say, 'What's your show about?' I say, 'Nothing.'"

George, still smiling, immediately affirms, "There you go."

Jerry pauses for a moment before nodding. "I think you may have something here."

While *The Cosby Show* dominated TV ratings in the 1980s with its celebration of meritocracy and its weekly moral lessons for American families, *Seinfeld* came along in the 1990s and playfully deconstructed the entire sitcom genre. In it, comedian Jerry Seinfeld plays a comedian named Jerry Seinfeld who, along with his three friends George, Elaine, and Kramer, traverses through the mundane slices of life that fill most of our days and calls attention to the absurdity of the experiences that make up modern life. Unlike *The Cosby Show* in the 1980s or the family-oriented TGIF sitcoms that were running in parallel with *Seinfeld* in its heyday, there were no moral lessons to be learned in *Seinfeld*. The protagonists were morally bankrupt, narcissistic, and devoid of any emotional intelligence.

Seinfeld became colloquially known as "the show about nothing" because, in the series, Jerry and George pitch NBC a "show about nothing" based on the show about nothing we're already watching.

Week after week, millions tuned in to watch a cast of characters who never changed, never grew, and never pretended to care about anything but themselves. *Seinfeld* reflected a worldview where nothing is sacred, sincerity is scorned, and ironic detachment is the norm. But can you really live without any story at all?

As we saw in chapter 1, *Seinfeld* wasn't alone in reflecting a new wave of cultural disillusionment with the moral certainty, meritocracy, and sincerity of the Modern Story. Something was happening in pop culture throughout the '90s that signaled the end of the Modern Story's role as the dominant guiding story. At first this shift felt liberating. We were being freed from the moralizing after-school specials and formulaic predictability of preachy sitcom endings. While you wait for a table at a Chinese restaurant, you might even whisper to your friend, "Hey, this is like that episode of *Seinfeld*," and laugh over how absurdly mundane most of your life is.

HOW THE MODERN STORY BROKE

The Modern Story portrayed life as a heroic struggle to chase after the truth and carve out your own destiny as you attempt to ascend the status ladder from rags to riches. But you're actually sitting near the coat rack inside a Ming's Garden, waiting for a table and wondering when this hero's journey thing gets to happen to you. *Seinfeld*'s nihilism felt comedic, but not every part of this anti–Modern Story energy felt so laughable.

After three or four hundred years as the dominant guiding story of the West, strong challenges and pent-up rage developed toward the Modern Story. Two world wars, a Holocaust, and an atomic bomb showed us that science and reason weren't going to lead us to some utopian paradise of pure rationality. Science could also wipe out all life on the planet with the push of a few buttons. Insert the *Oppenheimer* staring-off-into-the-void meme here.

And what if this notion that we all live in a meritocracy where anyone can pull themselves up by their own bootstraps isn't true? Or worse, what if it's just a clever new rat race those in power have created to keep the rest of us oppressed? Why do our modern hero stories tend to predominantly portray a certain type of hero over and over again? Luke Skywalker, Indiana Jones, Rocky, Batman—on and on the list of heroes goes. But what if you're not a white male? What if the rules of the game are stacked in the favor of white men to keep them in power? What if this Modern Story and all it stands for is just propaganda that covers up the real truth—that the only thing that matters is power? What if all stories are masking a play for power?

Nietzsche saw the inherent conflict between the Modern Story and the Christian womb that modernity had developed in. He knew that the separation of the sacred and the secular would inevitably lead to the death of the sacred along with the "death of God" in the West. But what would happen to Western civilization if we mutinied against God and kicked him off his throne?

Nietzsche believed that the theology of Martin Luther and later Reformers like John Calvin portrayed the relationship between humanity and God as God creating utterly depraved and helpless humans and—only through an act of sheer will—choosing which ones he will save. Because of this, Nietzsche also believed that what made God *most*

God was power. If God is power, when we kill God, something else must fill the vacuum of power.

In *Beyond Good and Evil,* Nietzsche wrote that "life itself is the will to power."[1] Moral right and wrong, and the stories that transmit those moral norms, are written by those who use their will to take and control power. Because God is dead and all that remains is the will to power, there are no real objective facts—only stories told by those in power. "There are no facts, only interpretations," Nietzsche wrote in his private journal in 1887.[2]

He planted the seeds of what would become a rival to the Modern Story, and this new story began to bloom in the elite centers of philosophy, literature, art, and even architecture in the mid-twentieth century. Postmodern philosophers like Michel Foucault, Jacques Derrida, and Jean-François Lyotard took up Nietzsche's project of deconstruction and expanded it. They argued that the Modern Story's self-proclaimed triumph of objectivity and reason was a lie masquerading as truth.

The Modern Story was right to question elements of the Traditional Story, but its deconstruction of tradition and the narratives that keep unjust authority in power didn't go far enough. If humanity were to truly be liberated from all forces of tyranny and enslavement, then we must learn to challenge all guiding stories. This was the beginning of the Postmodern Anti-Story.

THE ANTI-STORY

We can call this shift an anti-story because postmodernism did not present itself as just another competing guiding story. It was a sledgehammer that came to demolish all guiding stories. Like Morpheus telling Neo in *The Matrix* that the world he had been living in was a clever illusion developed as a system of control, postmodernism invited us to take the red pill and disbelieve all the stories we had been living in. The stories that fit the mold of both the Traditional and Modern Story share a coherent structure of beginning, middle, and end with a moral lesson and resolution. In the Postmodern Anti-Story the very structure of storytelling is questioned.

Take, for example, Christopher Nolan's *Memento,* where the film is told backward, scene by scene, with a protagonist and narrator who has short-term memory loss that forces the audience to question the reliability of the story they are watching. Without postmodernism you don't get films like *Memento* and *The Matrix*.

Postmodern philosophers like Foucault, Derrida, and Lyotard have never been mainstream household names, but by the 1990s their ideas were everywhere in pop culture. Power is always hiding in what we call *truth*. Because of this, the new heroes of the Postmodern Anti-Story weren't the ones who saved the world but the ones who *saw through it*.

For every value that the Modern Story championed, the Postmodern Anti-Story offered a critique. Unless you've lived in an Amish community cut off from popular culture, this anti-story has shaped you in some way—especially if you are Gen X, a Millennial, or Gen Z. Once you begin to see how the critique of each of the values of the Modern Story creates a new system of postmodern values, you will begin to understand what has been at the heart of the culture war in America since the 1990s and has only intensified since the rise of the internet, the smartphone, and social media. Not only that, but you will begin to realize how much this anti-story has shaped your own story.

Where the Modern Story celebrated the value of individualism, the Postmodern Anti-Story said that the autonomous self was an illusion. *Self* is a social construct, and your identity is shaped by systems of power and the stories those systems force you to believe. What we have come to believe is written by nature as an objective reality—even what it means to be a boy or a girl—is not objectively true but the result of cultural conditioning from those who hold the power in our schools, churches, and government.

The categories the Modern Story gave us to define ourselves, such as race, gender, and sexuality, are seen within the Postmodern Anti-Story as not being objective and fixed but fluid and relative to the cultural script you live in. If Martin Luther was a hero for rebelling against the unjust systems of his day, you can be a hero for rebelling against the labels people place on you. As the influence of the Postmodern Anti-Story spreads in the digital age, the act of self-identifying in defiance of cultural norms becomes the new mark of supreme heroism.

ANTIHEROES WHO SEE THROUGH IT ALL

In the Modern Story heroism was about taming nature, conquering evil, or ascending the ladder of meritocracy. In the Postmodern Anti-Story, the dragon you should set your eyes on slaying is the imposed identity that the Modern Story places on you. The moral triumph is the act of choosing your own identity as you risk alienation, ridicule, and exclusion from those you believe are still trapped in the Matrix. This is why it should come as no surprise that even the creators of the original *Matrix* trilogy, then known as the Wachowski brothers, eventually became known as the Wachowski *sisters* after each of them self-identified as women in 2008 and 2016.

The promise of the Modern Story and the American Dream was this: *You can make it if you try hard enough.* The circumstances of your birth don't limit your destiny. Success is earned. Whether it was Rocky Balboa becoming the heavyweight champion of the world, the undersized Rudy making the Notre Dame football team, or Hulk Hogan in the '80s yelling at us to train hard, say our prayers, and take our vitamins, our modern myths told us that all it took was enough grit, hustle, and willingness to grind to get to the top. But along came the Postmodern Anti-Story to mock meritocracy with all the subtlety of a jackhammer.

You're not really climbing a ladder; you're just running on a gerbil's treadmill that got a fresh rebranding. Meritocracy is exactly what the capitalists want you to think as you fill out another TPS report in your cubicle prison. For every Oprah story you can find, the postmodernists will be quick to point out millions of stories where being a woman and a minority doesn't even let you near the starting blocks, much less give you a fair race to the top. This race doesn't look like *The Pursuit of Happyness*, where a jobless man raising a child alone lands a career in high finance simply because he hustled harder; it looks a lot more like *Squid Game*, where desperate people are literally killing each other in color-coded tracksuits for a shot at climbing out of poverty. It's not just power all the way up the ladder; it's power that makes the ladder at all.

Pause for a moment and check in on your own narrative identity. When you feel burnt out at work, what is the voice in your head saying? Is it saying, "I just need to work harder to break through" (the Modern Story)? Or is it saying, "This whole system is a scam, and I'm just a battery fueling the machine" (the Postmodern Anti-Story)? The difference between those two voices determines which story is running as the operating system of your life.

Once again, within this critique from the Postmodern Anti-Story is an implied picture of what a good life looks like. If the ladder itself is an endless treadmill of oppression, the highest good you could pursue is the dismantling of the ladder. If the game is rigged, then the highest good isn't "succeed" but "reveal." Show how the game is rigged by the powerful, expose invisible privileges, and tear down the systems that perpetuate injustice.

While the Postmodern Anti-Story claims that all stories mask a play for power, an implied hero's journey still emerges from their critique. The hero of the Postmodern Anti-Story is actually the *antihero*. These characters don't ascend in heroic virtue or do-gooder status. They *unmask*. They expose the shadowy forces secretly running the show, like Morpheus and Neo in *The Matrix*. They deconstruct the story they're trapped in and break the fourth wall to expose its absurdity like Deadpool. Like Phoebe Waller-Bridge's *Fleabag*, these antiheroes may fail miserably and never redeem themselves through hard work and determination. They flex their postmodern superpower of being able to *see through* the story that's oppressing them.

What's a good hero story without a proper villain, right? And who could be a more wicked villain than the Wicked Witch of the West from *The Wizard of Oz*? I mean, her name should be a dead giveaway as to what side of the black-and-white moral divide she's on. Employing a legion of flying monkeys that kidnaps young girls might also be a red flag, right? Think again. What if she isn't evil—just green, misunderstood, and marginalized by the system? Oh, and she has a name. Elphaba.

That's the premise of the 2003 Broadway sensation-turned-Oscar-winning feature film *Wicked* (2024), and it is a quintessential example of the postmodern technique of *subversion*. Subversion is the intentional undermining or reversal of traditional or modern story structures, character roles, and moral categories to expose their hidden assumptions. If the antihero exposes the corruption or absurdity of the story they are living in, then maybe the same system that labeled a person a villain has misrepresented them and oppressed them with their labels. Subversion isn't about plot twists. Those have been around in our stories for millennia. Subversion in the Postmodern Anti-Story is about these questions: "Who gets to tell the story?" "Whose perspective is being privileged or centered?" and "What values or power structures are being quietly upheld behind the scenes of this narrative?"

Wicked is a subversive anti-story to *The Wizard of Oz*. *Oz* is a story told from the perspective of the winners, so of course it will marginalize and deem its opponents "wicked." Elphaba is deeply empathetic, and her empathy is employed toward the challenging of authority and the unmasking of injustice. She is labeled "wicked" because the system encourages people to fear and mislabel powerful women. *Wicked* especially resonated with women, not merely because of its compelling musical performances but because many women have felt that even the Modern Story, which encouraged rebels and reformers like Martin Luther, didn't allow for women to act in the same way as men. As one friend lamented to me years ago, "When I act like the men in my business meetings who are always speaking out about the way our corporate systems work, I get *awful* labels placed on me."

In *Wicked* it's the Wizard's regime that functions as the evil empire propped up by fear and propaganda. The alleged "wicked witch" isn't a villain. She's a misunderstood threat to the unjust social order. The gap between hero and villain is a gap in perspective. Instead of following Dorothy on her yellow brick road of moral clarity, we're invited to dance along in ruby slippers on a stage of moral ambiguity.

In the Postmodern Anti-Story, the heroes of the Traditional and Modern Story get questioned as villains, the villains of old like the Wicked Witch of the West or Maleficent get reframed as victims of trauma, and the antihero who spins the camera around to challenge the storyteller and the audience becomes the real hero. The Modern Story claimed to give us objective reality and, with it, objective morality. The Postmodern Anti-Story responds, "Yeah, that's just a con told by winners to justify why they keep winning." What it offers instead is a new kind of moral landscape with less black and white and more foggy grayscale.

The antihero of the anti-story isn't the person who builds something or who saves the day by killing the bad guys. They're the person who cynically tears apart the script page by page, telling everyone about the plot holes, and asking why the villain always has a foreign accent. In a world where every truth claim is an act, the most courageous thing you can do is question the director.

THE DEATH OF SINCERITY AND THE RISE OF IRONY

The undercutting of objectivity in the Postmodern Anti-Story also undercut sincerity. If the Modern Story had Hulk Hogan parading around an American flag and preaching virtue lessons after cage matches in 1986, only to have him reveal in 1996—while wearing a black "New World Order" T-shirt—that it was all a lie to sell tickets, that might turn all the little Hulkamaniacs into snakebit cynics. But our cynicism isn't all the Hulkster's fault. He's probably to blame for this young

Hulkamaniac's cynicism for a couple of decades or so, but pro wrestling just knew how to read which way the cultural winds were blowing (their whole business depends on being able to do that). What Hulk Hogan taught me in 1996 was that sincerely believing in something was not only naive but dangerous. After all, who wants to be a naive victim of oppressive power structures selling you propaganda for profit?

In the Postmodern Anti-Story, to be socially accepted we must constantly signal to the group that we are aware of the biases of the socially constructed story into which we were born. If that system conferred upon us special privileges, then we had better signal to the group that we know what those are lest we be complicit in some grand narrative of oppression. This creates an entirely new cultural grammar. I'm not just talking about highly ironic, insincere characters in *Seinfeld* or *Rick and Morty*; I'm talking about how we even talk to each other.

In this postmodern cultural grammar, the greatest sin isn't being wrong—it's being earnest and sincere without a proper disclaimer. You have to break the fourth wall like Deadpool and signal, "Hey, I know I'm in a socially constructed story here!" So we hedge. We preface. In the last decade or so, our prefacing feels like it has to keep getting longer and more specific: "Speaking as a cis white male, I realize this perspective might come from a place of privilege, but . . ."

Even if you've never felt the need to qualify your opinion with those specific postmodern-influenced labels, you may feel like every statement you make—even to your closest friends—must be wrapped in layers of caveats and given enough ironic distance to preclude you from any possible charges of naivety or complicity in oppression. Most often, this signaling isn't done with anxious prostration and quivering lips but with good ol' fashioned detached ironic humor.

This is why going back and watching an episode of *Full House* or *Boy Meets World* feels so cringe now. We're waiting for the characters to perform a Jim Halpert (*The Office*) side-eye to the camera every time something sincere or awkward happens to let us know that they know how ridiculous this all is. It feels foreign and strange to see someone not pad their convictions with strategic self-deprecation and ironic detachment.

Be honest: When was the last time you typed out a caption on social media or started to say something deeply sincere to a friend but then deleted it or cracked a joke at the end instead? That flinch you feel—the fear of being seen as too earnest, too naive, or too "try-hard"—is the programming of the anti-story affecting the very grammar of your daily interactions with others. *Cringe* is one of the primary enforcement mechanisms of the anti-story.

RELIGION ISN'T IRRELEVANT. IT'S OPPRESSIVE.

While the Modern Story tolerated the private practice of religion, the Postmodern Anti-Story treated traditional religion as another system of oppression, with its grand totalizing narratives being a force for colonial power and control. And typically it wasn't just any religion, mind you. It was usually Christianity, dressed in the vestments of colonialism, patriarchy, and moral absolutism, that got the harshest cross-examination.

In the Modern Story religion was something your grandparents did on Sundays. Harmless and benign, with a pinch of positive social utility—especially if you were trying to beat some Soviet Communists in a Cold War. Harmless enough so long as it stayed out of the science classroom and didn't try to vote. You could pray before school on "See You at the Pole" day, sheepishly thank a generic god at the Grammys, and slap an ichthus bumper sticker on your Ford Aerostar, but mostly religion was background noise, a placebo for those uncomfortable with the silence of the void.

But in the Postmodern Anti-Story, religion—and particularly Christianity—isn't just irrelevant. It's suspect. It's a power play disguised as piety. A totalizing narrative masquerading as universal truth. A justification for conquest, colonial expansion, heteronormativity, white supremacy, oppressive gender roles, cisnormativity, and a bunch of new categories of oppression that get rolled out every year like an iPhone update.

In the Postmodern Anti-Story, we were taught to critically reassess the impact of Christianity's totalizing claims on reality and to see it as another machine to rage against. From the Crusades and the Inquisition to Manifest Destiny and televangelists selling snake oil and apocalypse prep kits, the postmodernists weren't without a case. Being a "person of faith," as the modernists often called it, wasn't just outdated; it was downright oppressive.

The same Martin Luther who proclaimed that every individual had direct access to God without the need for institutional authority to act as mediators also wrote later in his life that Jews should have their synagogues burned, their homes destroyed, and their writings confiscated. Jonathan Edwards, the most influential preacher of America's first Great Awakening, whose sermon "Sinners in the Hands of an Angry God" transformed the cultural landscape of early America, was a slave owner who defended slavery's compatibility with a biblically informed faith. The radioactive pile of toxic-religion receipts felt like it could be stacked a mile high, from church sex scandals all the way down to a personal vendetta you might feel toward your evangelical mom who wouldn't let you read *Harry Potter* but thought God told President Bush to invade Iraq.

If you peruse TikTok, you can find an endless stream of critiques of Christianity ranging from personal church-hurt stories to scathing rebukes of historic Christian values and norms. In my teenage and young adult years, before the advent of social media, all the biggest films about faith in the zeitgeist were cynical critiques (aside from *The Passion of the Christ*, which was the outlier).

Saved (2004) parodied and skewered evangelical Christian school culture as a performative and hypocritical hub for repressive attitudes toward women. *Jesus Camp* (2006) was a documentary that followed a Pentecostal/Charismatic Christian Bible camp and exposed its practices of emotional manipulation and neoconservative political indoctrination of children. I mean, just ask yourself: If there's a pastor or a priest who shows up in the movie or series you're watching, are you expecting them to be a good guy or a bad guy? Bad guy every time, right? Which is kind of weird when, after watching every possible Netflix series with a pastor, you start to think, "I wonder if it is statistically true that every member of the clergy, aside from the dad on *7th Heaven,* is a sadistic serial killer?"[3]

Was this all just exposing the truth, or was it a nasty case of mean world syndrome, where the more we consume these stories, the more they distort our reality? When you hear the word *pastor* or *priest,* is the first image that comes to mind someone you know personally, or is it a cynical archetype from a prestige TV series or a viral news headline? How much of your current skepticism is based on direct experience, and how much might be a mean-world filter built by the stories you've consumed over the last couple decades?

It would be good to sit with those questions for a bit, but for now, let's at least take note of some startling data that should cause us to think deeply about the impact of the Postmodern Anti-Story on Christianity in America . . . and maybe even our own faith.

HOW THE ANTI-STORY CREATED A CRISIS OF FAITH

Remember that the rise of the Postmodern Anti-Story in popular culture began in the 1990s. From 1972 until around 1990, the number of Americans professing to be Christian hovered (with minor fluctuations) around 90 percent, while the religiously unaffiliated, or nones, and those in other religions split the remaining 10 percent. Then, somewhere in the early '90s, a precipitous decline among self-professing Christians began unlike anything we had ever seen in American history.[4]

Were people leaving Christian churches for Muslim mosques or Jewish synagogues? No. They weren't leaving for another traditional religion at all. They were just leaving . . . for *nothing*. Fast-forward to 2024, and there are more nones (28 percent of adults) than evangelical Christians (24 percent of adults).

Scholars and pundits of all kinds have proposed various theories to explain this decline of Christianity and the rise of nones. While I wouldn't claim there's a single inciting incident, we should not dismiss the obvious. The rise and spread of the Postmodern Anti-Story, which shaped us to be suspicious of any claims to an ultimate guiding story, spotlighted every instance of Christians behaving badly as evidence for the inherently oppressive nature of Christianity. It also provided social incentives to those who could best flex their antihero superpower of *seeing through* everything and has direct statistical correlation to the rise of the nones—the ones who claim to have no adherence to any ultimate guiding story. Over just three decades our culture changed the channel on all that preachy religious moralism and chose the show about nothing instead.[5]

To put it plainly, why would we be shocked that when a new guiding story came along and told us not to believe anything, more people than ever started not believing in anything?

But if humans are inherently storied creatures and we can't shut that off, what happens when we try to live in a show about nothing? And isn't the claim that "all stories mask a play for power" a story too?

What happens when we kill our guiding stories?

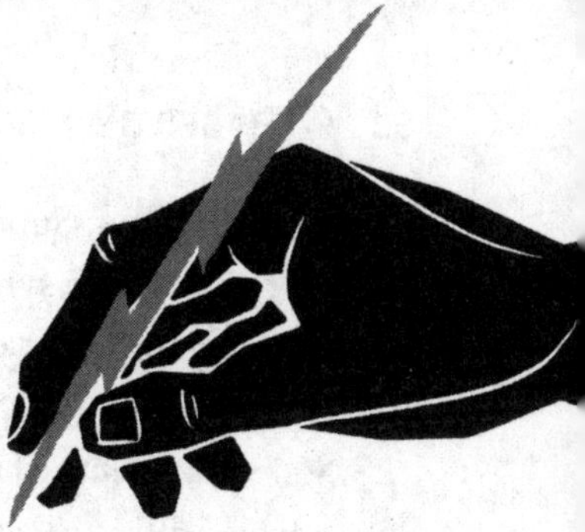

CHAPTER 5

The Death of Superman

I can only answer the question "What am I to do?"
if I can answer the prior question
"Of what story or stories do I find myself a part?"
Alasdair MacIntyre

As we've learned already, nearly every culture since the dawn of time has created hero myths. The hero myth is not just entertainment; it discloses what the culture prizes as its highest aspiration for its people to reach toward. The hero of these stories functions as an *archetype*—a symbolic pattern that captures the deep reservoir of shared human experience and imagery and helps people make sense of the world. This archetypal hero both shapes and discloses a culture's zeitgeist. The ancient Sumerians had Gilgamesh. The Greeks had Achilles and Hercules. In America our greatest archetypal hero is Superman. So when the zeitgeist shifts, you can expect our Superman stories to shift.

Like those demigods of old, Superman is endowed with strength and might that appeals to the primal instinct of boys who long to be strong and brave. Yet countless strong-man myths and comic-book heroes never ascended to the same heights of cultural significance as the Man of Steel, whose symbolic appeal goes far beyond the imaginations of prepubescent boys. Superman is the quintessential, archetypal symbol of America's unique synthesis of the Modern Story's values, including the lingering influence of Christianity in our culture. And in 1992 we killed Superman.

Superman debuted in *Action Comics #1* in 1938 and was conceived into a world of historic turbulence and uncertainty. The United States was still struggling under the weight of the Great Depression. Adolf Hitler had seized total control of what would become Nazi Germany. Japan was expanding its imperial ambitions into China and Southeast Asia with brutal atrocities like the Nanjing Massacre. The world was headed toward another great war, with tensions reaching a boiling point in Europe and Asia in 1939. The zeitgeist was shifting.

With anti-Semitism on the rise, Jerry Siegel and Joe Shuster, sons of Jewish immigrants to America, created a tale of an alien immigrant sent out from a dying world like Moses down the Nile, only to be rescued by a couple of Midwestern farmers instead of an Egyptian princess. Superman's adoptive parents were salt-of-the-earth Kansas Methodists (this particular religious detail was revealed in later stories) who instilled in him the highest values of the Modern Story and their weekly, church-going faith.

Superman became the bulletproof patron saint of a uniquely American mythos built on the scaffolding of Christian messianic hope and Enlightenment grit. While Europe increasingly de-Christianized after World War II and gave itself to a more thoroughly disenchanted Modern Story, we held on to our mythical moral exemplar, who was raised with all of the heartland values you'd expect from decent Midwestern Methodists.

In 1978 we were at another critical juncture with a seismic zeitgeist shift in the balance. Amid a Cold War of competing guiding stories at a civilizational scale between the United States and the Soviet Union, the iconic values of Superman were shared with the world on the big screen. *Superman: The Movie* was syrupy and sincere, iconic and hopeful—all of the essential ingredients of the Americanized blend of the Modern Story with the Christian values of humility, self-sacrifice, and compassion toward the least of these. But by the mid-1980s, even as the guiding story of our civilization was winning out against the Soviet vision, there were signs that our culture was beginning to question whether this Superman icon was genuine or propaganda.

By 1986, writer Frank Miller, deeply shaped by postmodern thought, portrayed Superman as a loyal stooge to a corrupt presidential parody of Ronald Reagan, galavanting around the world as America's foreign-policy policeman in the seminal *The Dark Knight Returns*. From the assassinations of John F. Kennedy and Martin Luther King Jr., to the Vietnam War, to the emerging allegiances between influential televangelists like Jerry Falwell and those in power in the Republican party during the Reagan years, Americans were becoming increasingly suspicious that the Superman myth was exactly what the postmodernists had claimed about stories like this—at best, it was antiquated and naive; at worst, it was propaganda.

Just as the archetypal symbol of our culture's highest ideals emerged in the zeitgeist on the precipice of World War II with the birth of Superman, in the early 1990s the shifting zeitgeist of American culture decided it was time for Superman to die. In 1992 DC Comics released *The Death of Superman*. Superman was beaten to death with his tattered cape strewn across a pole on the front cover as if it were the remnants of an American flag after a lost battle. It quickly became one of the best-selling comics of all time and over the next three decades produced a new kind of archetypal story that reflects the symbolic ache at the core of our meaning crisis: "Superman's dead. Now what?"

SITTING AT SUPERMAN'S FUNERAL

Before we rush to answer the "Now what?" question, we should sit for a moment at Superman's funeral. Not just to mourn the death of a fictional alien in red and blue spandex but to linger in the ache that made his death, and maybe your own loss of faith in all that complicated symbol stood for, feel necessary. Because what draws most people into the orbit of the anti-story isn't reading obscure French philosophers. It's pain and grief.

It's a parent dying young. A prayer that goes unanswered. A trusted pastor or mentor who turns out to be a predator. A friend who goes off to fight a war that your church told you was "God's will" and comes back broken. A voter's guide handed to you by your pastor who stamps God's approval on a corrupt politician or a flawed partisan platform. Suddenly the American flag that stands next to the pulpit at your church starts to look a little different. A pastor runs off with a girl in the youth group, and suddenly the next pastor who takes his spot doesn't look like he is wearing a cape. All of these connections between the place you live, your culture, and your faith start feeling like different rooms in one home, and this home feels like it's collapsing.

The cognitive scientist and philosopher John Vervaeke calls this experience *domicide*, which literally means "the killing of home." But what Vervaeke means by this term isn't the destruction of the physical house you live in; rather, it's the felt destruction of one's sense of home in the world. It's the feeling of existential and spiritual dislocation that happens when the story you've been living in no longer feels tenable.

The death of Superman is a symbol of our culture-wide sense of domicide. It is the sense that somehow all these individual experiences of loss of faith, distrust of power and authority, and disenchantment have all been networked together into some kind of collective experience that *we* have lost our home. And it's not just that we've lost one spiritual home and are moving to another, as if we found a superior iteration of Superman to look up to; it's also a sense that *no* home is available to us.

As Vervaeke highlights, in an experience of domicide, we lose our sense of

ORIENTATION—our sense of direction in life
BELONGING—the feeling that we are anchored in a community with a shared history
NARRATIVE IDENTITY—the internal story of who we are and how we fit in the world
ANCHORS OF MEANING—things that help us experience meaning, like rituals, symbols, and shared practices[1]

This absence creates in us feelings of alienation, anxiety, confusion, and nihilism. No one wants to sit in these feelings for long. We might be tempted to skip all the eulogies for Superman at the funeral and rush on to the "Now what?" part of our lives, but rushing through the process of grieving can create a new set of problems. We all want to regain a sense of agency, like we have a significant role to play in the purpose of life within a coherent story. Still, our pain can easily pull us in the direction of something that makes us feel like we have agency in the world, even if it's not part of a coherent story. The danger then is that we can become addicted to an illusion of meaning, a *pseudo-meaning* that eventually spirals into further pain and devastation.

Ian Harber, author of *Walking Through Deconstruction*, experienced domicide as an unexpected string of successive suffering and unanswered questions about God, the world, and his place in it, which completely disoriented his narrative identity. The story he had been raised in felt incoherent, and the life strategies he had been given seemed broken.[2]

It was pain on top of pain—profound alienation from community giving way to the ineffectual pursuit of *pseudo-meaning*. In that place of despair, the anti-story had a powerful gravitational attraction. Life did feel incoherent. Maybe there were no heroes, only differing degrees of power and privilege to tear down. Ian, and many others who have shared in a similar experience of domicide, found a momentary illusion of meaning by becoming the quintessential protagonist of the anti-story: the antihero. But as we'll see, that illusory sense of purpose and significance is not sustainable. The antihero isn't enough.

THE RISE OF THE ANTIHERO

As we learned in the last chapter, the Postmodern Anti-Story attempts to offer people who have felt the pain of oppressive power a new heroic calling: Become the antihero who *sees through* the lies. This turns your grief into a call to action, and there is something empowering about that, as if you've suddenly regained your agency. You won't let the system define you or control you. Superman might be dead—or worse, a lie—but you've got a job to do. Your new "Now what?" becomes making sure that no one else gets hurt by naively believing in all that symbol stood for. Deconstruction becomes your new mission.

Like Jesse Eisenberg's Millennial-inspired iteration of Superman's nemesis, Lex Luthor, in *Batman v Superman: Dawn of Justice* (2016), those who have been hurt by power often come to see God and all who stand for power as symbols of oppression. As Lex says to Superman in the film's climactic confrontation, "I learned at an early age, no man in the sky intervened when I was a boy to deliver me from Daddy's fists and abominations. I've figured it out way back: If God is all-powerful, he cannot be all good. And if he's all good, then he cannot be all-powerful."[3] The pain pulls us into the anti-story's orbit. Maybe all power works like Tolkien's One Ring, corrupting all who wear it. Maybe all stories are just about power, and if so, my new calling is to tear them all down.

Since the 1990s, our fear that not only is Superman dead but all that he stood for is a lie has created a new archetype in the zeitgeist. We can call it the *dark Superman archetype*. The dark Superman archetype—figures like Homelander (*The Boys*), Injustice Superman (DC), or Omni-Man (*Invincible*)—is a powerful subversion of our once-beloved icon. These characters look like saviors, speak the language of justice, and wear the cape, but it all masks the real truth that they're tyrants, sociopaths, or broken gods. Our new "Now what?" becomes playing the part of the antihero who *sees through* the Superman veneer and exposes the Homelanders of the world for what they really are.

Homelander is one of the most compelling of the dark Superman archetypes. His character was first created in 2006, amid a post–Patriot Act and War on Terror America, but he has been popularized more recently through Amazon's series *The Boys* (2019–present). You'd be hard-pressed to find a more meme'd, cape-wearing character on the internet, which, in our age of social media, reveals the potency of a symbol. In public this evil parody of Superman, who dons a star-spangled costume and cape and possesses all the powers of the Man of Steel, feigns the sincerity and moral fortitude of Superman in order to mask his psychopathic, narcissistic desires.

He is the anti-story's anti-Superman, a heat-vision-wielding anti-Christ who shows up at evangelical outdoor music festivals to campaign for God and country without an ounce of authentic care for either. He is what many legitimate victims of the abuse of power in the name of God believe about all authority and all stories that make totalizing claims. To them, Superman isn't just dead; he's propaganda.

Exposing every Homelander feigning as Superman becomes the new righteous cause of those who have been hurt by power and believe that what Superman stood for was naive or propaganda. Deconstruction feels heroic, and raging against the machine gives a sense of meaning to those who rightly want to see the Homelanders of the world exposed and dethroned. Yet the Postmodern Anti-Story and its effort to assign some sense of meaning in life to the task of *seeing through* lies and unmasking evil leaves us with a fascinating dilemma.

When *Wicked* subversively challenges us to consider if the Wizard of Oz was the real villain, or when Tyler Durden in *Fight Club* convinces a bunch of disenfranchised men that the system is turning them into soulless consumers, it cannot be because *all stories* mask a play for power. These are stories too, right? If you felt like leaving your religious upbringing when you found out about Martin Luther's anti-Semitism or because you went to a Christian school that felt a little too much like the movie *Saved*, it cannot be because all stories are wrong. The story that "all stories mask a play for power" is *itself* a story.

THE ANTI-STORY IS A STORY . . . JUST NOT ONE YOU CAN LIVE IN

In fact, it was an unexpected group of deconstructionists trying to somehow live within the Postmodern Anti-Story who were among the first to find out that there's a fundamental problem with trying to live in a show about nothing. This surprising critique came from feminists in the 1980s. At first these feminists—who felt that the Traditional Story, the Modern Story, traditional religion, and the very symbol of Superman were propaganda intended to protect the story of male dominance—found postmodern thought an ally in their cause. The *patriarchy* was just one guiding story masquerading as objective truth. So the anti-story helped them attempt to tear down that narrative, which they saw as masking a play for power. But there was a problem. As Canadian scholar of postmodernism Linda Hutcheon noted, "Feminists in the 1980s were among the first to attack postmodernism's complicitous form of critique, its tendency to deconstruct cultural monoliths but never to reconstruct."[4]

If *everything* is just a power play, if *all* truth claims are socially constructed, then on what basis could the feminists fight for their vision of equality and liberation? And if the work of deconstruction never ends, then what's to keep the deconstruction from coming after the very idea of being a woman? These feminists weren't content with dismantling the old world. They wanted to build a new one. They could not simply run away from one world—they needed to run *toward* another. Herein lies the fundamental problem with only having an anti-story.

We only know that Homelander is wrong because, deep down, we believe Superman or something even better than Superman must be true. For a story to be a lie, there must be a true story to compare it to. What is it that makes colonialism, slavery, racism, and misogyny all wrongs to oppose? It cannot be that all we have are varying shades of devils and darkness competing in a ruthless contest of domination for the throne of hell.

An anti-story by itself is incoherent. Every deconstruction is parasitic on a deeper construction. You can't name something as unjust, harmful, or hypocritical unless you're already operating with a standard of justice, health, or integrity. Augustine said evil was just a movement away from good. Gregory of Nyssa said it was a sickness we know only by a standard of health. C. S. Lewis said we only call something crooked because we've glimpsed the straight line.[5]

The Postmodern Anti-Story depends on a moral memory, however faded, of the very story it tries to unravel. It wants to throw out the Superman myth as naive and oppressive, but it still needs a better Superman to measure him against. And that's the paradox: Every anti-story points—however reluctantly—toward a truer, better story that must still be hiding behind the curtain.

You want to expose the Homelanders of the world? Good. But life cannot be an endless *seeing through*. That pursuit offers us pseudo-meaning. What happens when that sledgehammer of deconstruction is your only tool and your entire life becomes consumed with swinging at every story as the next wall to knock down? At first, a life given to demolition may feel righteous and even liberating. Swinging the sledgehammer of deconstruction feels like an act of catharsis for your grief. But keep swinging it long enough, and that catharsis can quickly turn into a state of cyclical cynicism. Now the cynical antihero has become your new identity, especially if you've found others who also love to wield the same sledgehammer.

Even those who don't completely abandon their religious community, family, or previous circle of friends can take on as a badge of supreme heroism their ability to call things out and "speak truth to power." The incentives around swinging a sledgehammer can become incredibly lucrative when one can easily coalesce an online community around a podcast or TikTok account that's all about seeing through and unmasking.

You might try to start an exvangelical church or join an activist group that mobilizes people around a shared mission of deconstruction, like the ragtag group of antiheroes led by Homelander's chief thorn-in-the-side, Billy Butcher, in *The Boys*. Finding a shared vision of something to oppose is a powerful catalyst for community action, and we humans are community-oriented creatures. But building a community around an antivision never works in the end. Sure, you might enjoy a year or two of solidarity as you bond over shared grief and pain. Many times we can't even find people to share in our questions, anger, or loss, so finding someone else who says "I see you" can feel like all we need to hear. But eventually that sledgehammer will run out of things to swing at *out there*, and the engine of cynicism and deconstruction will turn inward on the community and cause it to implode.

Ian Harber and millions just like him have lived this journey and realized the vanity of going through life only wielding the sledgehammer. If we're to find a sense of home again, we need to have eyes that do more than just *see through*. We must be willing to risk a wager of hope that there is something to *see to*.

SETTING DOWN THE SLEDGEHAMMER OF DECONSTRUCTION

The sledgehammer has its place, but the problem is that sledgehammers don't build homes. You have to live *somewhere*, and you can't tear down forever. Eventually you're left sitting in the rubble of deconstruction, exposed to the elements of anxiety, disorientation, and spiritual homelessness. The old structures may have had their flaws and even some rot in the beams, but they gave you somewhere to live. You've seen through the Homelanders and maybe even appropriately raged at some machines that were evil empires, but *now what*?

Eventually you realize that with all you've torn down, you're cold, alone, and staring into the void, realizing that there's no such thing as a show about nothing. You can't just go through domicide after domicide. You have to live somewhere. As C. S. Lewis wrote in *The Abolition of Man*:

> You cannot go on "seeing through" things forever. The whole point of seeing through something is to see something through it. . . . To "see through" all things is the same as not to see.[6]

Staring into that void is frightening. When you look around at the rubble and realize there is nothing to shelter you from the elements, you begin to see that these stories warn us of what will happen on the other side of the death of Superman. Over and over we see in these archetypal stories a warning that what comes to fill the story void is most often far worse than what we discarded. When Superman dies, something else always rushes in to fill the vacuum of power. It might be worse supermen, malicious new gods, or, worst of all, Darkseid (Superman's supreme nemesis and archetypal symbol of evil personified), who comes to us wielding his "anti-life equation."

We cannot live in an anti-story with only an antivision. What we really want isn't endless deconstruction but *reform* that is oriented toward a vision of our highest good. We are increasingly realizing that what filled our story void after the chaotic sledgehammer of postmodernism leveled it all has been anti-life. We can never actually be godless and storyless. Just look at what has rushed in to fill the void and offered us anti-life and pseudo-meaning as our new gods—political extremism, culture wars, endless sexual revolutions, and sophisticated social media algorithms that monetize our outrage and cynicism. The anti-story has deformed our souls.

But what if we could take the desire to *see through* that the Postmodern Anti-Story baked in to us and apply it to seeing through the anti-story itself? Could we dare to hope that there may actually be something to look up to? Could we, without a hint of naivety, sincerely hope to find a story worth living in that could liberate us from our cynical prisons?

WHAT COMES AFTER DECONSTRUCTION?

David Foster Wallace, who perhaps more than any author in my lifetime had the antihero's superpower of *seeing through*, had begun to *see through* the anti-story itself and predicted there would come a day when the zeitgeist would shift beyond the Postmodern Anti-Story. Just as American pop culture began to experience a postmodern zeitgeist shift, Wallace saw what was coming. In 1993 he wrote:

> The next real literary "rebels" in this country might well emerge as some weird bunch of "anti-rebels," born oglers who dare to back away from ironic watching, who have the childish gall actually to endorse single-entendre values. Who treat old untrendy human troubles and emotions in U.S. life with reverence and conviction. Who eschew self-consciousness and fatigue. These anti-rebels would be outdated, of course, before they even started. Too sincere. Clearly repressed. Backward, quaint, naive, anachronistic. Maybe that'll be the point, why they'll be the next real rebels. Real rebels, as far as I can see, risk things. Risk disapproval. The old postmodern insurgents risked the gasp and squeal: shock, disgust, outrage, censorship, accusations of socialism, anarchism, nihilism. The new rebels might be the ones willing to risk the yawn, the rolled eyes, the cool smile, the nudged ribs, the parody of gifted ironists, the "How banal." Accusations of sentimentality, melodrama. Credulity. Willingness to be suckered by a world of lurkers and starers who fear gaze and ridicule above imprisonment without law.[7]

Wallace tragically took his own life before he could see his prediction come true. That day is happening right now. There is another zeitgeist shift in our midst, and if you look closely, there are signs of it everywhere. Cynicism is passé. Detached irony is being traded in for post-ironic sincerity. And with it all there is a fresh hope of recovering meaning in a coherent story that can hold our deepest longings for purpose and significance.

Superman has returned.

In January of 2023 a new *Superman* movie was announced, promising a fresh reboot of America's most important mythological hero. Tracking the cultural vibe shift, my sense was that we would get a Superman who would be the antithesis of the cynical, dark archetypes. Our exhaustion with the anti-story and all that it had done to our souls and culture was reaching a breaking point. In December 2024, with a July 2025 release date on the horizon but before the first trailer was even released, I predicted on social media that we would be getting a new aspirational Superman who "will make all of the cynical Homelander tropes instantly feel passé."[8]

We were ready to break free from our meaning crisis and go beyond postmodernism. In that same month I told people to expect a *metamodern* Superman who would be "Christopher Reeve + Ted Lasso + a dash of Waymond [from *Everything Everywhere All at Once*]" where a wholesome and sincere Man of Steel would be juxtaposed "against characters who embody the ironic, self-aware cynicism of our postmodern age."[9]

If you've seen *Superman* (2025), you know that's exactly what we got. In Wallace's words, this Superman was an "anti-rebel." In one viral scene, this new Superman pushes back against the cynicism of Lois Lane and tells her that, just maybe, his sincerity and kindness are "the real punk rock."[10]

Maybe you still have enough of that postmodern proclivity toward suspicion to make you go, "Cool. That's one example. Where else can I find evidence of this vibe shift?" Let me show you where to look, what it means, and why the time is *now* for all of us to start reconstructing again.

CHAPTER 6

Everything Everywhere

> Irony has only emergency use. Carried
> over time it is the voice of the trapped
> who have come to enjoy their cage.
>
> *Lewis Hyde*

It's a pretty common occurrence for people who follow my work to reach out to me and say, "Paul, you've got to check out this movie and tell me what you think it's about." Back in 2022 I kept getting the same message about the same movie over and over: "Paul, have you seen *Everything Everywhere All at Once* yet?" That DM would usually be followed up by, "It might be the weirdest movie I've ever seen," with subsequent efforts to find appropriate film comparisons. "It's kinda like *The Matrix* but also completely different. It's doing Marvel multiverse stuff, but in a totally different way." This all intrigued me enough to give it a try.

Weird was right. But *Everything Everywhere All at Once* was more than weird. Sure, you have multiverse martial arts, talking raccoons, hot-dog fingers, sentient bagels, and characters who become rocks that just sit there in the silence of an alternate universe devoid of all living things, but this didn't feel meaningless. In fact, it seemed like it was trying to say quite the opposite. And that thing it was attempting to say touched a cultural nerve. Contrary to some people's opinion, you don't win Oscars (which this film did) just for being weird.

Absurd? Yes. Maximalist and bizarre? Absolutely. It really was everything everywhere. If *Crouching Tiger Hidden Dragon*, *The Matrix*, *Back to the Future*, and *Rick and Morty* all got poured into a blender and cranked on high, you might get something approximating *Everything Everywhere All at Once*. Yet it also had something else that was difficult to name. Somewhere between the family screaming matches about the mundane aspects of life, such as laundry and taxes, and an existential black hole of nihilistic despair shaped like an everything bagel threatening to consume all of reality, the film pulled off something unthinkable to all those who had been caught up in the typical anti-story irony and cynicism for decades.

Sincerity.

Not naive and cringey Jessie-becomes-addicted-to-caffeine-pills episode of *Saved by the Bell* sincerity. Not the Hallmark Channel kind either. It was the kind that stung you a bit because you weren't expecting it and didn't know how much you missed it. The mechanism it used for getting at sincerity? Irony.

For all of us shaped by the popular media of the Postmodern Anti-Story, irony became our native tongue. This cultural grammar saturated everything. It dripped off the screen in every Tarantino film. It colored every line of dialogue in David Fincher's big-screen iteration of *Fight Club*. It's the unmistakable dialect of Deadpool, Larry David, and Rick Sanchez. Even our news turned into an ironic meta-performance in programs like *The Daily Show* and *The Colbert Report*, playing as a wink-and-nudge version of the thing it was pretending not to be. All of this irony was in service of *seeing through* and maybe giving you a good *Seinfeld*-esque laugh at how absurdly meaningless it all was if you weren't the type to burn the whole system down.

On the surface, *Everything Everywhere All at Once* uses all that ironic postmodern grammar—fragmentation, absurdity, multiverse overload, the impossibility of objective meaning—but then it does another seemingly postmodern move to postmodernism itself. It subverts our expectations for irony to be in the service of cynicism and instead uses irony to say something sincere. It takes you *through* the irony to get at sincerity. The film begs the audience to grapple with the question, "So we've *seen through* everything. Now what?" And instead of giving us an antihero who watches the world burn to the ground while listening to a Pixies song, we get a teary-eyed immigrant mom hugging her daughter in a laundromat.

That immigrant mother, the film's protagonist, is named Evelyn Wang, and Evelyn is having an existential crisis. Her laundromat is failing, her marriage is cracking, her daughter is slipping away, and the IRS (perfectly personified by Jamie Lee Curtis in a joyless beige turtleneck) is breathing down her neck. Evelyn is in a pressure cooker of midlife malaise when she's suddenly yanked sideways through the multiverse and told, quite unceremoniously, that she's the chosen one. But not because she's particularly brilliant or brave. She ain't exactly the Neo or Anakin Skywalker chosen-one type. (Uh . . . thankfully. Right, Jedi younglings?) She's been chosen precisely because she's failed at everything.

From there the film spirals into a kaleidoscope of absurd alternate realities. The villain at the center of it all is her own daughter. Well, technically, it's her daughter Joy's multiversal doppelgänger, Jobu Tupaki, who's created an everything bagel—yes, really—that sucks in every possible meaning only to force all who behold it into the nihilistic conclusion that nothing matters.

But the character who holds the key to saving the multiverse isn't really Evelyn. It's Waymond. Her soft-spoken, kind, fanny-pack-wearing husband. The guy everyone, including Evelyn, has overlooked. Waymond isn't powerful. He's not wise. He's not exactly Superman, but he isn't the Billy Butcher postmodern antihero either.

He's not trying to *see through* it all. He's not raging against the machine. He sees the absurdity, the chaos, and the disappointment, and he still chooses kindness, sincerity, and love. In one of the film's most disarming scenes, Waymond says, "When I choose to see the good side of things, I'm not being naive. It's strategic. It's how I've learned to survive everything. I know you see yourself as a fighter. Well, I see myself as one too. This is how I fight."[1]

Waymond isn't the naive modernist, and he isn't the cynical postmodernist. He's something else: an unexpected archetypal hero of a new vibe shift in the zeitgeist, neither retreading modernism nor keeping us indiscriminately swinging our postmodern sledgehammers ad nauseam. This shift seeks to mine the best insights from both, while still taking us beyond the modern and the postmodern. You could call it *metamodern.*

The Postmodern Anti-Story taught us to *see through* everything—the institutions, the myths, the heroes in capes, and the parents in pews—but it never taught us what to do afterward. There was no afterward. There wasn't a coherent story to build toward. It handed us a sledgehammer and said, "Nothing is sacred—swing away, kid." Jobu Tupaki is what happens when you reach the logical endpoint of deconstruction: Everything becomes so relativized, so ironized, so disassembled, that everything everywhere becomes meaningless. The everything bagel is not just a postmodern punch line. It's the abyss that stares back at you when you've unraveled every story until all you're left with is static. And into that static walks a new kind of wholesome hero.

He doesn't arrive with a revolutionary manifesto or metaverse-sized punch. We might still be a little too suspicious of that kind of power. Waymond wields goofy optimism, an open heart, and a quiet, stubborn refusal to give up on kindness. He doesn't *see through* the world. He takes C. S. Lewis's advice and *sees into* it. He's the boring rebel that David Foster Wallace hoped would one day replace our cynical antiheroes.

THE METAMODERN SHIFT

This is just one of the flavors of the metamodern shift. Again, it is not a naive return to syrupy sincerity that keeps its head in the sand while Homelander flies around heat-visioning the vulnerable. It's a *new sincerity* that's been through the fires of irony and cynicism and come out the other side still believing. Not because it ignored the pain but because it refused to let the pain close its heart.

While this shouldn't be interpreted as a ringing endorsement of *Everything Everywhere at All Once* (none of the pop culture references in this book are personal endorsements . . . well, except maybe for *Seinfeld*), it should be considered an important cultural artifact. The film doesn't offer a coherent new story to rebuild within, and finding that story will be necessary so we don't settle for more pseudo-meaning that leaves us empty again. But what it does point to is a rope that seems to be getting dropped down to us in our pit of postmodern despair, with a voice on the other end that reassuringly says, "There is a way out."

The idea that something would shift in the zeitgeist, taking us beyond postmodernism, has been around since the days of David Foster Wallace. What audiences felt in *Everything Everywhere All at Once* could also be felt in trace amounts in the earlier work of Wes Anderson movies like *The Royal Tenenbaums* and *Fantastic Mr. Fox*, in post–season one episodes of the US version of *The Office*, and even in Wallace's *Infinite Jest*. Each of these examples uses postmodern irony, which might normally be associated with the sound of a sledgehammer whirling through the air aiming at the next system to be deconstructed, but tries instead to get its audience to sincerely look at something within themselves that might be broken.

In *The Royal Tenenbaums*, it is broken trust and fractured relationships in a family. In *The Office*, it is the pivot from existential apathy in a soul-sucking office job to learning to love the people you're trapped in the system with. In *Infinite Jest*, the characters who most rely on incessant irony are emotionally crippled and miss the authentic connection that those in addiction recovery—who are learning to speak the truth, however awkwardly—experience as freedom. Again, none of these are saying, "Let's go back to the Modern Story!" Instead, their message is, "We've lost something in the anti-story that we need to recover."

It's almost as if the Wes Andersons and David Foster Wallaces of the world started to see that with all the Postmodern Anti-Story had torn down, there was still something broken that we could not escape: *us*. This insight was the beginning of the bridge out of the anti-story. Some might call it late-stage postmodernism or early-stage metamodernism; regardless of what you call it, there were signs of hope that we might not have to settle for being swallowed up by an everything bagel of nothingness. We knew we could expose facades but couldn't heal what was fractured in us.

THERAPY CULTURE AS SUBSTITUTE SALVATION

With this late-stage postmodern / early metamodern shift came the rise of therapy culture. *Therapy culture* is a term that describes the growing presence and influence of therapeutic language, values, and practices in everyday life. When my grandad returned from fighting in the Pacific Theater in World War II, no one told him he had trauma and should talk with a therapist. Even when I was a kid, there was this idea that people who saw psychiatrists were one step away from living in a padded room while wearing a white straitjacket for the rest of their lives.

Therapy culture is new, and it's everywhere. I'm thankful those stigmas have changed, but I do wonder why therapy culture is exploding just when the anti-story seems to have run its course. When we demolished all the old stories we were once living in and still felt an absence of meaning, we turned inward. In an effort to find a new hero's journey not seen in the Traditional Story or Modern Story—one that didn't keep us trapped in the endless, empty cycle of the snarky antihero—we created a new kind of increasingly self-aware, therapeutic hero. If we were still suspicious that all stories masked a play for power, we couldn't turn to a pastor or a priest to help us navigate our own narrative identity, as would have been the norm for pretty much anyone in my grandparents' generation and older in America. We would want to find a guide who was supposedly neutral and narrative-free. We would want to tap into that category created by the Modern Story. We would want someone *secular*.

The "neutral" secular therapist becomes the ideal guide in a landscape where people are wary of any single, overarching narrative. If we remember that one of the most important implied values of the Postmodern Anti-Story was self-authorship, then the therapist becomes the guide to helping us figure out the problems in our own story and author a new one. Because the therapist is perceived as free of any guiding-story commitments, we feel safe to work on the things that need healing within us without the pressure to conform to a larger, guiding story. As a pastor confessed to me years ago, "It feels like the therapist is taking my job."

Even our superhero myths began drawing from the grammar of postmodern irony found in a Tarantino movie, applying it to this new metamodern quest to feel something sincere and creating a new hero's journey we could call "therapy as salvation." Take even a couple of examples from the post-*Endgame* installments of the Marvel Cinematic Universe. In *Thor: Love and Thunder*, the story isn't about a hero's quest to save the world as much as it's about Thor trying to process his grief, identity loss, and cosmic-level burnout. He's not storming Olympus or Asgard to war against other gods so much as he's trying to find himself after experiencing years of tragedy, coming to terms with his ballooning dad bod, and dealing with a drinking problem we probably shouldn't be chuckling at.

Or take *WandaVision*, Marvel's bizarre, highly self-aware love letter to classic television that turned out to be less about sitcom nostalgia and more about a woman who's trapped in a cycle of unresolved grief. Wanda, aka the Scarlet Witch, doesn't fight a world-ending big baddie like Thanos. Instead, she fights denial, trauma, and the aching impossibility of ever bringing her family back from the dead. It's highly ironic and self-aware, breaks the fourth wall, and exhibits all the other typical hallmarks of the postmodern aesthetic, yet it clearly isn't an anti-story. It's an effort at something sincere. It's trying to point to the possibility of leaving perpetual deconstruction for some form of reconstruction.

Even the quintessential ironic, cynical antihero of the postmodern age, Deadpool, began to shift into this metamodern, therapeutic hero's journey to find something sincere and meaningful. Deadpool was supposed to be the end of the aspirational, Superman-styled hero story—a mercenary mutant who breaks the fourth wall, cracks dirty jokes about the absurdity of living in a story, and murders whatever sacred cows remained in the superhero genre. Maybe more than any other comic book archetype, he is the one who can *see through* everything. He's even self-aware enough to know that he's just a comic book character.

When *Deadpool* (2016) first hit theaters, it felt like the apex predator of the Postmodern Anti-Story: a hero who wasn't even pretending to be heroic anymore. Wade Wilson, aka Deadpool, knew it was all a sham. Heroism, love, redemption—that syrupy Superman stuff was dead. Instead of trying to save the world, he invites us to sit with him on the couch, sharing a chimichanga while telling us obscenely dirty jokes laced with the darkest combinations of cuss words the human ear has ever heard, all the while laughing at our ridiculous efforts to find meaning.

But *Deadpool* also made an unexpected contribution to the cultural conversation through its own metamodern pivot in *Deadpool 2* in 2018. The quintessential antihero who could out-cynic everyone else was quietly, awkwardly dragged into something dangerously close to . . . sincerity. After losing the love of his life, Deadpool doesn't just double down on nihilism—he cracks, genuinely grieves, and stumbles his way into discovering that the only way forward isn't endless snark or another fourth wall–shattering joke. It's an epiphany that feels completely unexpected for a character whose mouth would make Andrew Dice Clay blush. Deadpool comes to the realization that Christ is the highest ideal he could aim for when it came to finding meaning and healing his trauma. Seriously. And these connections are incredibly explicit (in more than one sense of the word).

MARVEL JESUS

Thus far, this is probably at the top of my "not a personal recommendation for family friendliness" list of movies, so I may need to break this down for you in lieu of you not doubling the amount of filthy language you've heard in your lifetime through a single viewing of the film. One of the first meta-clues of the Merc-with-a-Mouth's cross-shaped longing comes early in the movie when Deadpool tells his taxi driver, "Now I'm talked about in the same sentence as Jesus." After which he pans to the camera to break the fourth wall and remind the audience that the first Deadpool movie was a huge R-rated box office success: "*Passion of the Christ*, then me. At least domestically. We beat them overseas, where there's no such thing as religion." Maybe it's just typical braggadocious banter, but there's more.

After the death of his girlfriend, Deadpool finds himself yearning for new meaning in his life and discovers a young boy with mutant powers who is being abused. Deadpool has always been the antihero without a moral compass, but now he wants to be a hero. Maybe caring for and protecting this kid can help heal his grief and make him a hero? But he doesn't really know what the true shape of heroism looks like. Sitting at a bar, he laments to a bartender named Weasel that something in him needs to change:

Deadpool: I'm not gonna abandon this kid. He's never had anyone, ever. I need to be selfless.

Weasel: Yeah, but what does that mean?

Deadpool: It means I'm gonna save Russell. Maybe I couldn't save Vanessa, but maybe I can save a robust teenager from New Zealand.

Weasel: Yeah, but what I mean is, like, the word "selfless." I literally don't know what that means.

Deadpool: *Jesus Christ.*[2]

It may seem like he's just taking the Lord's name in vain as he is apt to do, but it's another meta-clue to the audience that the selflessness Deadpool deeply aspires to beneath the layers of cynicism and irony can find no higher archetype than Christ. In the climactic resolution of the film, Deadpool sacrifices himself again to save the kid caught in the spiral of vengeance and abuse, only to be resurrected like Christ. Deadpool, the avatar of irony, is forced to look at the story of Christ not as a punch line but as the only archetypal narrative big enough to make sense of his pain. His healing isn't found in another dirty meta-joke or in endless cynical deconstruction. It's found in becoming a stand-in for Christ and bleeding for the sins of someone else. The lesson he learns carries over into the sequel *Deadpool and Wolverine*, as he once again saves the day by laying down his life, returning from the dead, and boldly announcing to the audience in his typical irony-laced, Ryan Reynolds–paced quippiness, "I am Marvel Jesus."

These movies aren't getting recommendations from Focus on the Family anytime soon, and I wouldn't expect any Deadpool-themed Vacation Bible Schools popping up at churches in the summertime. The point isn't to see this as a Christian movie that will air after *The Chosen* marathon. The point is that there are signs that our culture has begun to wake up to the reality that perpetual deconstruction and cynicism is a prison that left us feeling alone, and in this isolation, as we felt the pressure to self-author a story, we began to realize the brokenness *out there* was also *in here*. If *in here* is to "get right," what does that look like?

Having left or deconstructed the institutions and stories that once afforded us pathways to reconstruct, and still feeling stung by the experiences in which those institutions and stories had been used as tools of oppression, we were left to find guides who could claim neutrality in the story wars and could help us self-author our way out of our meaning crisis. But as we did this, our cultural stories also revealed another ache: What direction should we even self-author toward?

SELF-AUTHORING CAN'T SAVE US

Therapy culture has come with pros and cons. On the one hand, it has helped us to realize that "the system" is made of people and that broken people make broken systems. Good luck raging against the machine when the people raging are just as messed up as the people in the machine. Learning what needs fixing in us is good. It probably would have been good for my grandad to process with someone some of the pain he endured fighting in World War II. Therapy culture has destigmatized sharing genuine pain and loss. It's also helped those who have difficult brain conditions, which impact their quality of life, be less likely to endure isolation and social ridicule. And it's signaled an awakened desire throughout our culture to find some possible pathway for reconstruction. We are allowing ourselves to sincerely hope again.

However, in the cultural stories that have flooded not only the Marvel movie market but also the Disney and Pixar universe, the hero's journey has portrayed therapy as salvation, setting us up for another round of pseudo-meaning that doesn't heal the world. In *WandaVision* the entire world and every person in it seemingly exists solely for the purpose of Wanda's therapy. Other people are just ornamental in our self-authored story. Entire multiverses rise and fall so that we can process our trauma. We may not be deconstructing anymore, but a self-authored story isn't a habitable story you can share with others.

In *Moana*, the beautiful Pacific Islands scenery and culture is a backdrop to a hero's journey that is still trying to navigate where the holdover values from the Modern Story and the Postmodern Anti-Story fit in our quest to be healed from our sense of meaninglessness. Moana rejects externally imposed expectations, listens to the voice within, and uncovers a deeper identity that was always there, waiting to be named. It is an effort to draw on the modern and the postmodern and to *synthesize* a way forward toward some sense of salvation. Borrowing from lessons learned in *Wicked* and *Maleficent* about misunderstood monsters who were victims of oppression, Moana learns that the land is healed not by slaying the monster that possesses it but by speaking to its pain and offering it therapeutic healing.

Moana's hero's journey becomes a mix of Joseph Campbell and Brené Brown, with her call to adventure being an inner voice that beckons her to reject the outer expectations placed upon her in order to discover her true identity. To find her self-authored salvation, she must learn to trust her deepest self. Once she learns to trust her deepest self and helps the monster Te Kā to recover its true name, which has been suppressed, life and flourishing return to the dead island. If we can just move past the external labels others have placed on us and author our own lives, salvation will come.

Several years ago, a friend of mine was struggling to navigate a relationship with a colleague who had come to believe that her inner voice was beckoning her to self-author a better story for herself. There was no abuse or infidelity in her marriage, just common middle-class married life struggles, and yet she wasn't feeling like her "true self." So she ditched her husband, abandoned her kids, and moved to a place in the world where it's always sunny. Is she happier now? She actually might be. But you know who isn't? Definitely her kids.

What if self-authoring your own notion of salvation leads to someone else's hell? Maybe you've already come to realize, through the trials and errors of your own life or from the pain that came with someone else self-authoring a story that didn't consider yours, that there has to be a better option than endlessly critiquing every story or just inventing your own.

THE LIMITS OF SELF-AUTHORING

The vibe shift that began to bubble up in the zeitgeist, which has been trying to find a way beyond the cynicism and endless deconstruction of the Postmodern Anti-Story, was born out of our meaning crisis. As we attempted to *see through* everything that was making our story feel incoherent and devoid of purpose while robbing us of our significance, we started running out of external options to blame and started looking inward. Maybe admitting to a therapist, "I need help," gave us permission to believe that not all sincerity was naive.

"There is no truth" gave way to "Find your truth." And to be fair, that's probably a slight upgrade. Especially for those crushed under the weight of shame, abuse, or generations of trauma, the notion that your story doesn't have to end with what was done to you can feel like a breath of resurrection. But for this all to not lead to more pseudo-meaning, it has to be more than "your truth."

If you are the only author of your story, who holds the red pen when you go off the rails? The therapist is not neutral. They are not free from all stories. For them to help you name what is broken in your family, your marriage, and your thoughts, there must be some standard of health for them to aim you toward. If there's anything we should have learned from postmodernism, it's that none of us are storyless. Only a story that starts from goodness allows us to name what moves away from the good.

Self-authoring can't tell you what the good life is. It can't decide whether it's better to lay down your life for another or to protect yourself at all costs. This can only be known by adhering to a story that comes from outside ourselves. The story must *transcend* us.

Ironically enough, this is where Ryan Reynolds's big-screen iteration of Deadpool actually gets it. This loud, broken, cynical antihero believes that not only is a better story possible, but it's necessary to find real meaning in life. We're not getting healed by deconstructing another system. Ironic, self-aware snark is a self-protection mechanism, not a door to salvation. If we're going to get out of this abyss, we need an archetype to aim toward. A Superman. A Christ. A story outside ourselves that can hold us when our own authorship fails.

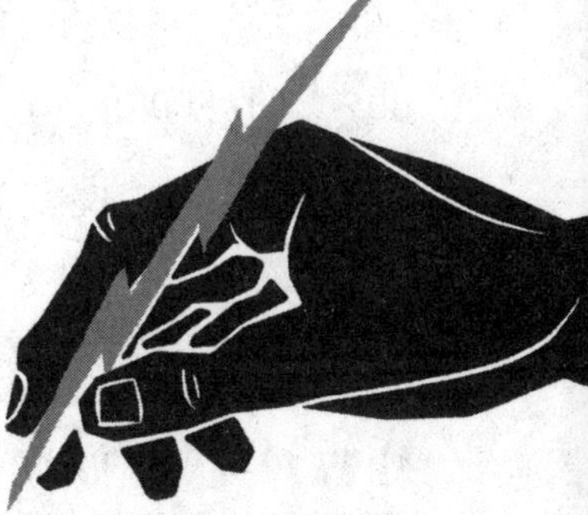

CHAPTER 7

Can You Take Me Higher?

To live ironically is to hide in public.
Christy Wampole

Realizing that there's never a show about nothing and seeing the limitations of our ability to self-author, we've started to understand that we need a story outside ourselves. A Superman. A Christ. An archetype to aim toward. But maybe the path to finding that story doesn't always start with a flash of revelation or a mountaintop moment. Maybe it sneaks up on us in the rituals we didn't realize were shaping us, in the songs we thought were jokes, in the things we mocked before we learned to love them. What if we are shaped more by what we *do* than by what we *think*? And what if sometimes what we do, even if we start doing it ironically, rewires our loves before our minds catch up?

In a world that's long since traded capes for cynicism, we don't always reach first for the Superman archetype or the Christ figure when we go looking for a story to reconstruct our lives within. Sometimes the strangest, most seemingly ironic things become sincerely sacred again. Sometimes they start reshaping us into a *higher* story before we even know what that story is.

The very symbols we mocked in our irony-soaked phase have started to shimmer with new resonance in this metamodern shift. Because what we need isn't always what we expected. And who would have expected that the soundtrack for our zeitgeist shift would be a turn-of-the-millennium, power-ballad rock band that had once symbolized everything overwrought and uncool? Who could have seen it coming that what was once the epitome of *cringe* would be a metamodern doorway out of our cynical prisons?

Well, I did.

I was the guy who predicted that the band Creed would make a comeback. And boy, did that comeback exceed even my expectations.

SOMEHOW CREED RETURNED

But before I help you see what I saw and explain why the unexpected resurgence of a maligned millennial neo-grunge band should matter to you, let me take you back a few decades to a minivan full of angsty teenage boys caught in the collision of the fading Modern Story, the rising Postmodern Anti-Story, and the peculiar counterculture of '90s evangelical youth groups.

The year was 1997, and I was sitting in the back seat of a minivan filled with my best friends from my Christian high school and church youth group. All of us hovered in that liminal generational space between geriatric Millennials and young Gen Xers. We had been shaped by the cultural forces of Seattle's grunge sound and MTV, but we were also old enough to remember what it was like to watch *Rocky IV* without a tinge of postmodern irony.

Mixed in with all those colliding values of the dominant macrocultures of the time was our full immersion into the unique evangelical-youth subculture, which was attempting to tap into the countercultural spirit of that era and redirect its focus toward making teenage Jesus freaks. If the phrase "wiggled around like marmalade jelly" means anything to you, then you probably could have been sitting in that minivan with us and gotten along just fine. I don't remember where we were going, but I remember the moment when a new song came blasting over the airwaves from Detroit's "new rock alternative, 89X."

It had hints of Pearl Jam and early Stone Temple Pilots, but the lyrics sounded like something we could get away with playing at church youth group. In our particular subculture, listening to secular music was frowned upon, so each of us was always on the lookout to discover Christian rock bands that could appease our parents and youth pastors.

This disapproval of secular music was so intense that I remember one day in my small Christian school when the entire middle school and high school gathered for an emergency assembly. A crime had been committed, one serious enough to warrant classes being canceled and the church's senior pastor coming in to address us. Someone had carved "Rage Against the Machine" into a school desk. The framing of the offense was not around the destruction of school property but that someone in the school liked satanic secular music. So we learned to trade homemade mixtapes that were filled with the latest from Tooth and Nail Records and other Christian rock record labels, but we also snuck in the occasional Bush and Green Day songs that wouldn't get us into noticeable lyrical trouble if our parents walked into our bedrooms.

Was what we were hearing through the minivan stereo a new Christian rock band? We all waited patiently for the radio DJ to uncover the mystery band's name: "And that was Creed with 'My Own Prison' off their debut album."

We drove straight to the closest record store (though I have no recollection how we knew to get there—or anywhere, for that matter—without Google Maps), grabbed our first Creed CD, and started learning every guitar riff on the album with our imitation Fenders and Metal Zone distortion pedals. In a cultural moment that was navigating the tensions between the sincerity of the Modern Story and the irony of the Postmodern Anti-Story, Creed was belting out ballads with full-throated sincerity—all without a tinge of irony.

Their music was religiously tinged but ambiguous enough to land them spots at the top of the Billboard charts and Woodstock '99 instead of playing at Creation Festival with the Newsboys and DC Talks of the Christian rock subculture. At first, it seemed like everyone believed. Sincerity hadn't completely fallen out of fashion yet, and Creed was awesome.

Not long after their rise to the top, Creed was exiled from the kingdom of cool. The peak of their cultural ascent was a 2001 Dallas Cowboys halftime show on Thanksgiving Day. Lead singer Scott Stapp wore a Dallas Cowboys jersey. Cheerleaders adorned the stage, and Cirque du Soleil–style shirtless, bald acrobats descended from the rafters, flying across the football stadium on white, flowing bedsheets. Camera cutaways to scenes from the September 11 aftermath played as the band sang "My Sacrifice" with dancers spinning around and raising star-spangled banners. It was all the Modern Story had stood for and a last-gasp effort as the zeitgeist shifted to the postmodern as if to say, "Wait, Superman's not dead yet!"

The Turkey Day spectacle was the beginning of the end for Creed. The vibe had shifted. Critics and hipsters labeled them "corporate butt rock." The cultural tastemakers collectively decided that Creed's brand of stadium-sized sincerity was just too much. Too earnest. Too melodramatic. Too *cringe*.

In the Postmodern Anti-Story, where sincerity was suspect, Creed was public enemy number one. The band became a punch line by the mid-2000s and an object of ridiculous memes in the 2010s. The sincere "Creed is awesome!" gave way to the postmodern critique of "Creed is corporate buttrock," which eventually shifted to the ironic "Creed is awesome, lol" memes where "*werth erms werd erpen*" was pasted on top of Scott Stapp pictures mocking the singer's unique and earnest vocal stylings in their former hit "With Arms Wide Open."

The ironic "Creed is awesome, lol" jokes and memes were a way to culturally signal that you weren't one of those naive fools still stuck in the Modern Story. Legends of backstage tirades and behind-the-scenes diva behavior from the lead singer only seemed to justify what everyone was already feeling about those who outwardly present themselves as sincere Superman types. Remember—it's all just covering up the real Homelander behind the facade.

But then in 2023, just as other signs of a new vibe shift in the zeitgeist were emerging, I began to notice a strange new trend happening online. The Creed memes were beginning to change. The winks at the camera started to fade. The air quotes around "Creed is awesome" started to disappear. People stopped laughing and started belting, "Can you take me higher?" in a way that was neither indicative of the original naive sincerity of 1997 nor the purely ironic mockery of the 2010s. It was a *post-ironic sincerity*.

Then it dawned on me. That thing we saw hints of in Wes Anderson movies and *Everything Everywhere All at Once*—the idea of going through irony to get at sincerity—was happening with Creed. This band was beginning to show signs of a metamodern revival. So in the late summer of 2023, I took to my podcast and social media to announce a bold prediction: "There is going to be a major resurgence of Creed in the next year."

This prediction wasn't fueled by a secret desire to have all those Creed guitar riffs I'd learned in high school and college become socially acceptable again. It wasn't fueled by a nostalgic longing to be back in simpler times, riding in my friend's parents' minivan. I saw in Gen Z TikTokers, who had lived with the irony, cynicism, and deconstruction of the Postmodern Anti-Story, a yearning to feel something again—something *wholesome*. Perpetual mockery and detachment, combined with a global pandemic that only deepened our isolation in ways we're still coming to terms with, had exacerbated a generational crisis of meaning.

That detached irony was a self-preservation mechanism. Irony gave you just enough emotional distance from the vulnerability of actually feeling something dangerously earnest. But as we began to move beyond postmodernism, this detached irony, which we use to ensure that we can keep *seeing through* every story without being attached to any story, wasn't enough to heal our own brokenness and satisfy our longing for meaning.

The same realization—that Waymond from *Everything Everywhere All at Once* might be on to something that ironic cynicism misses—began to draw twentysomethings, who had only ever ironically listened to Creed as a form of signaling their detachment, to start belting at the top of their lungs, "Can you take me higher?" And when this post-cynical wave started to break, it wasn't just an obscure TikTok trend.

By the fall of 2023, headlines began to appear during the Major League Baseball playoffs that the Texas Rangers were blasting Creed in their clubhouse to generate positive vibes before the game. By the American League Championship Series, the Rangers were proudly sirening Creed's "Higher" throughout the ballpark at every home game with forty thousand fans singing along, propelling them to an eventual World Series championship. The players attributed their ability to overcome a midseason losing streak and eventually win the championship to the way the song changed the entire vibe of the team.

Dan Solomon, writing for *Texas Monthly*, described his fascination with the Rangers' culture completely changing because of these Creed musical rituals—and how something was changing within him too. When "Higher" first came out in 1999, Solomon was a self-described punk rocker working at a record store, and like most punk rockers caught up in the anti-story aesthetic, he detested the syrupy sentimentality of Creed. He wrote in an October 2023 article entitled "How the Texas Rangers Taught Me to Stop Worrying and Love Creed":

> Stapp sang like Eddie Vedder and the band thumped like Soundgarden, but without any of the subversion that those creators used to balance out the inherent pomposity of their bombastic rock and roll stereotypes. Pearl Jam's songs asked listeners who wanted to rock out to meaty riffs to identify with women and marginalized characters; Chris Cornell had enough self-awareness to poke fun at

the rock star–as–messiah image by giving his band's songs names like "Jesus Christ Pose." Stapp, meanwhile, belted out lines like "The world is headed for mutiny / When all we want is unity" with a straight face, and he dressed like Moses cosplaying as a pirate who'd just discovered a treasure chest full of leather pants. The grunge acts Creed aped sought to subvert rock tropes; Stapp embraced them. It's still impossible to imagine him using the word "irony" unless he was grasping for an adjective to describe Iron Man.

But also: Who cares about any of that now? The dream of the nineties is long dead . . .

Hearing "Higher" sung at Rangers home games during the team's seven-game ALCS victory over the Houston Astros also helped me understand something else: Creed's guilelessness is an asset, not a hindrance. The band's songs don't have the subversive artistry of their grunge predecessors, but sometimes that's not what you're after. Sometimes, you want to put one hand over your jersey-clad heart, raise your other fist to the sky, and sing along to a hook that's big enough to hold 40,000 other voices.[1]

In the fall of that same year, Creed announced a full-blown reunion tour via a highly self-aware social media video. In 2024 Creed had their highest-grossing year as a band. Songs that were over twenty years old were topping the charts again and continued to do so well into 2025. My prediction couldn't have been more spot-on.

POST-IRONIC SINCERITY

But why should any of this matter to you?

The Creed resurgence isn't just a weird blip in the nostalgia algorithm like people swapping out their skinny jeans for baggy cargos. It's another sign of the seismic zeitgeist shift. For a generation whose native tongue was irony and cynicism, embracing Creed with straight faces and full lungs is the kind of cultural rebellion that would have made David Foster Wallace proud. But "rebellion" isn't really the best word to describe this anymore. Sure, when the status quo is ironic detachment, belting out, "Hold me now . . ." and the specific distance you are from "the edge" might feel like a strange inversion of the angsty, anti-story mobs that burned down Woodstock '99 while chanting the postmodern mantra "[Bleep] you, I won't do what you tell me." But framing it as rebellion, as if rebellion is inherently an act of valor, is still processing this through the lens of the Postmodern Anti-Story (and to some degree, even the Modern Story).

What writer Dan Solomon felt as he let go of his cynicism wasn't a desire to channel his old rebellious, punk rock energy at a new system. It was something more than rebellion. It was the epiphany that "guilelessness was an asset, not a hindrance."[2] It was the realization that there was some higher good that he had missed and now wanted to look up to. Sure, there was some *seeing through* component to the epiphany he and millions of other metamodern Creed enjoyers came to. In particular, they needed to *see through* the lie that perpetual ironic detachment and angry cynicism were for their own good, but this is much more akin to looking up beyond the clouds to get a glimpse of the sun. And yes, I'm sure there's a clever "Higher" pun in there somewhere.

What comes after the *seeing through* stops and we finally set our gaze upward? It's worship. If that word feels a bit loaded for you, what's really behind the meaning of that word is two questions: What beyond me is worthy of my attention? What is the ultimate concern that my life should be oriented toward?

Because if we're going to find the real meaning our souls are looking for and not just more pseudo-meaning, this can't be about swapping targets for another rebellion. It has to be about retiring the sledgehammer altogether and asking if there's something worth building again. Something worth singing about. When you see crowds of Gen Zers and younger Millennials throwing their arms around each other at a Creed concert, singing lyrics that sound like a youth group altar call without a trace of irony, it might look like a crowd of David Foster Wallace's anti-rebels. But framing the highest good as rebellion is still framing it within the parameters of the anti-story. What you're witnessing now is more like a pilgrimage. It is a movement *toward* something better.

What's happening now is the rumbling of a culture-wide conversation about whether it's possible to believe in something that sounds like salvation. This is about repentance. A cultural *metanoia*—a Greek word sometimes translated as "repentance" that means "a change of mind" or "to think beyond." It's a longing to go upward and *higher* (there's the pun). If someone tells you, "Hey, you know Creed isn't musically and lyrically as artistic as Radiohead," you go, "Cool. Don't care."

This is embracing the cringe.

If you're a digital native—someone born into the digital age where Wi-Fi, smartphones, streaming services, and social media have always been a part of your life—you may have a greater fear of being cringe than of environmental apocalypse, civilizational collapse, or totalitarian AI takeover. The very fact that I, as a married adult male in my forties, have used the word *cringe* is already causing my teenagers great consternation.

Cringe is the cultural cardinal sin of the post-internet world. When any moment of your life could become a social transgression that gets posted online for the world to mock, you become hypervigilant at making sure you avoid that hell at all costs.

If you're a high school basketball player in a gym full of smartphones, the last thing you want is a failed dunk attempt in warm-ups to go viral and for the whole world to mock you. So you learn to go about half speed, barely jump off the floor, and throw up some half-hearted layup attempts to clearly signal, "Yeah, I'm not really that into this." If you go a little too earnest in a class presentation, all it takes is one cynic with an iPhone to blast your naivety all over the internet so the world can heap its scorn and shame on you. So running like an antivirus software in the back of your mind is the ever-vigilant cringe-avoidance program.

Avoiding the cringe is motivated by our fear of social rejection, but living in this fear hasn't given us what we are actually looking for. It just tried to get us away from the thing we want to avoid, which isn't the same thing as finding what we need. What we all deeply need is *connection*, and detachment keeps us from it. In fact, there can be no satisfaction of our longing for significance without connection to people we can be significant to.

Pause for a moment and ask yourself, "Where have I lost the real connection I know I need because of my fear of being *cringe*? Have I stopped myself from sharing something I made with others because I didn't want my sincerity to be seen as naivety?" You may even want to jot down a few examples that come to mind and unpack those later.

There can be no doubt that the way this whole Creed thing got back into the zeitgeist after decades of irrelevance was because of the irony and the memes. Maybe for some people it still stayed in that zone of ironic detachment, but here might be the most meta-ironic thing of all: This meme-sharing compulsion might have backed us in sideways to the one thing we were looking for but didn't know we needed: *connection*.

You might have queued up "With Arms Wide Open" on the party playlist as a bit, with friends rolling their eyes while mouthing the words in a faux gravelly voice. You might have turned it on during a road trip with a friend as a gag that got you both laughing, but then somewhere along the way, when you reached to change the track on the playlist, your friend reached out and stopped your hand. You weren't just *performing enjoyment* anymore. You were now enjoying.

HOW RITUAL CHANGES OUR STORY

This is precisely what philosopher James K. A. Smith meant when he wrote, "You are what you love . . . and you might not love what you think," in *You Are What You Love: The Spiritual Power of Habit*.[3] How do the guiding stories and values of your surrounding culture become part of your narrative identity? It is not just watching, listening to, or reading a story that shapes your soul. Storytelling itself is powerful, but *ritual* is how you inhabit a guiding story and how the story inhabits you. Ritual is the process of rehearsing and reenacting the story through symbolic participation in it.

Our rituals shape us more than we're aware and bring us into alignment with a story, oftentimes before our brains can even name the propositional claims in the story we've started to believe. When you keep returning to the thing, even if you don't know what to make of it yet, your body starts to memorize its rhythms. You participate. You sing. You gather. You connect. When you act as a character in the story, you are performing a ritual that puts that story into you.

Smith called these rituals—which happen in everything from singing the national anthem before an NFL game or cosplaying as a *Star Wars* character at Comic-Con—"cultural liturgies." Like the liturgy you'd experience at church on a Sunday morning, the goal of these rituals is to form in you a sense of what's worth loving through participating in that story.

You do the liturgy over and over again, and before your rational mind has time to protest, you realize your affections have been rewired. In the age of cringe and Creed, ironic participation becomes embodied liturgy, and that liturgy begins to aim your heart in a new direction. You accidentally fall in love with the thing you joked about because it was never really about the thing—it was about being human in a crowd of other humans, hungry for meaning, for joy, for connection . . . dare we even say, *Communion.*

The Texas Rangers get stuck in a batting slump and completely change the vibe of their team by changing their rituals. In this case, they embraced the cringe of singing along with the guilelessness of Creed, and it became a new liturgy. After repeated exposure and practice, it got into their cultural DNA. Singing Creed together started driving deeper connection, but not the kind of connection people tend to momentarily experience around deconstruction together. That type of connection eventually implodes because it requires having something to be against, and those targets always turn inward. Promise. The Rangers' Creed connection was hopeful, wholesome, aspirational, and—please forgive me for another pun—it really did take them higher.

Platinum-selling songwriter John Mark McMillan experienced a similar metamodern metamorphosis that completely reoriented the story he was living in. McMillan had been born and raised in Charismatic church contexts that prioritized singing power ballads to God that would make Creed blush. No one was going harder after sincerity and communion in music than Charismatics in the '80s and '90s. McMillan began his songwriting ventures in the context of these Charismatic Christian communities, which eventually led him to bring his songs of sincere worship to open-air stadiums filled with sixty thousand people singing his lyrics.

With a gift for melody and an aesthetic sensibility that resonated with more than just the Christian subculture, McMillan began touring larger clubs and venues that had major crossover appeal beyond the Christian subculture. He longed to say things that the current subculture's container didn't seem to have room for.

By the mid-2010s, McMillan started to feel a pull into the anti-story's orbit. Looking back on the world he had been raised in, he realized that some real Homelanders had started to make him wonder if Superman really was dead. He wouldn't have called it a full-blown deconstruction, but some sledgehammers were certainly flying inside him. The songs he once sang with utter sincerity were starting to feel naive and maybe even painful to sing.

Then in 2023, his wife went through five difficult surgeries, his father-in-law was dying of cancer, and his father suffered an aneurysm. Just the kind of life events that can make whatever remains of the story you were living in completely collapse on you. But for McMillan, it didn't. He describes the strange inversion of the anti-story in his life that year:

> See, the universe can be cruel, and doesn't care if you're on the verge of a panic attack. You still have to do all the dumb normal stuff. Walk the dog. Make the breakfast. Drive the carpool.

So I was forced to slow down.

It was hard. There was no future to dream of in 2023, and I didn't know what to do with myself. I tried to be productive. It was futile.

But I noticed something—I caught myself singing little Charismatic praise choruses to pass the hours. Over time, they began to pleasantly haunt my days . . . and in the process, I remembered how good it felt to love God without ego or cynicism. It was like stumbling home and seeing it again for the first time."[4]

THE LOWLY AND DESPISED THINGS

You see, this isn't about Creed. It's about a spiritual shift that seems to be animating a generational movement to rebuild within a better story. There's a Bible verse I used to hear back in my youth group days that has somehow stuck with me in between all the lectures about secular music and saving it for marriage:

"But God chose the foolish things of the world to shame the wise; God chose the weak things of the world to shame the strong. God chose the lowly things of this world and the despised things . . ."[5]

I can safely say from my years of graduate-level theological studies that the apostle Paul wasn't prophesying the Creed comeback tour. But it might be entirely possible that, just maybe, the archetype we're searching for happens to use foolish things all the time. Maybe you rolling down the windows of your 2008 Ford F-150 and belting out with your closest friends, "Hold me now! I'm six feet from the edge and I'm thinking . . . maybe six feet ain't so far down" is the kind of lowly and despised thing that just might be crazy enough to break the nihilistic spell.

If we are ever going to be able to reconstruct into a story that accurately orients us toward that which should be of ultimate concern and can fulfill our insatiable longing for meaning, we will have to move beyond the ironic detachment of the postmodern age and embrace the cringe.

Sincerity is dangerous. Opening ourselves up to authentic connection comes with risk. If you're waiting for the modernist, objective, third-person perspective on reality before you get back into a sincerity and wholesomeness that could make Superman blush, then I'm afraid you might be getting stuck on naivety or cynicism.

Embracing the cringe isn't denying that it's cringe. It's not throwing out the valid critiques of postmodernism, which highlighted the ways in which our beliefs and sense of identity are shaped by social constructs. It's not saying, "I have the perfect view from nowhere!" It's the realization, "I have to live somewhere, and I'd like for it to be with other people."

This isn't about aesthetic tastes or musical redemption arcs. It's about *soul formation*. About becoming the kind of person who is shaped not by fear but by joy. Who is willing to look up again, to feel again, to find meaning again. Because the price of staying safely ironic is a life with no anchor. And the cost of caring out loud? Well, that's how Communion begins.

Cringe is the cost of caring out loud. It's the cost of vulnerability, and vulnerability is the cost of authentic Communion. Our longing for connection, communion, meaning, and hope within a better story is bubbling up all around the culture. We're not deleting postmodernism entirely, and we aren't just going back to modernism, but we are realizing that something somewhere has been lost. To rebuild and move forward, we must retrieve the wisdom we discarded.

This retrieval isn't nostalgia in the shallow sense of sentimentality or escape. It's a deeper kind of remembering, a re-membering of the dismembered. In the rubble of domicide, we're beginning to dig through the ruins of what was torn down—not to live in the past but to carry something sacred from it forward. As we'll see in the next chapter, there is a form of psychologically healthy nostalgia. Healthy nostalgia doesn't keep us stuck; it helps us reintegrate the parts of our story that were true, good, and beautiful.

As postmodern storytelling constantly subverted the stories of the past that gave us a sense of home, this new metamodern vibe shift began to subvert our expectations for subversion. When subversion became a tired trope, a wave of stories emerged in the zeitgeist that inverted the subversion, offering a healthy sense of nostalgia and signaling that we were ready for a culture-wide reconstruction.

In one of the best signs of the times, the sequel to a Reagan-era fighter-pilot movie made us feel something again. If, when watching the film, you felt tears starting to stream behind your aviator sunglasses and experienced the urge to throw your fist in the air to a power ballad driven by a familiar guitar solo, then maybe something in your soul was telling you, "I'm ready to rebuild."

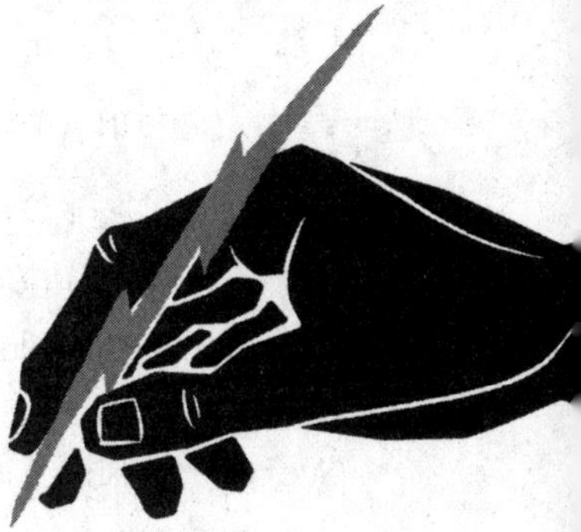

CHAPTER 8

This Is What Movies Used to Feel Like

> We travelers, walking to the sun, can't see
> Ahead, but looking back the very light
> That blinded us shows us the way we came,
> Along which blessings now appear, risen.
>
> *Wendell Berry*

In 2022, as waves of the pandemic lingered on, the movie theater appeared to be on death's door. Not only was the fear of public gatherings still a concern, but because of culture-wide domicide, it appeared that our cultural stories were stuck in a cycle of endless movie reboots and sequels. Perhaps we were searching through our old stories for one on which we could stabilize ourselves. Sure, you might think all that is just a greedy cash grab, but that still doesn't answer the question of why the big studios thought people still wanted to see the old stories.

They knew nostalgia was playing some role in our cultural moment and wanted to meet that demand, but they misread the spiritual shift and didn't realize what we were really aching for. We had been without a shared story home, and perhaps we all sensed a subconscious need to return and retrieve what we had lost. The 2010s had generated a seemingly endless supply of reboots, prequels, and sequels, but the problem was that while we were searching through our old stories from the past, we were simultaneously still stuck in the anti-story mode of deconstructing and subverting those stories.

We were looking back but still trying to *see through*.

A prime example of this was the *Star Wars* sequel trilogy. *Star Wars* had been one of our most influential and important cultural myths, so the very thought of seeing Luke Skywalker, an archetypal bastion of hope and light, again drove millions to the theaters in the late 2010s. But instead of seeing an older, wiser hero of unconquerable virtue that we could all aspire to, we met a disillusioned and depressed hermit who had abandoned the Force and his friends and needed moral lectures from an inexperienced teenage girl to eventually snap out of his funk. It was a classic case of postmodern subversion.

So when the first trailer for a *Top Gun* sequel hit the internet, I fully expected a similarly subversive treatment of Tom Cruise's Maverick. It was 2022, and we had all lived through not just a pandemic but an intense period of activist culture, #MeToo, cancel culture, and race-related struggles in the culture war. All of these movements were like a hypervigilant Homelander detection system, where the antihero who can *see through* and deconstruct was awarded the highest levels of social reward for being the most vigilant. By 2021, it felt as if every corporation, pro sports team, movie, streaming series, and commercial had to signal their postmodern credentials. Maverick was just the kind of "toxic masculinity" that Gillette commercials had warned us to be deeply suspicious of while trying to sell us their razors and shaving cream. So what happened next may have been just as unexpected as the return of Creed.

INVERTING OUR EXPECTATIONS FOR SUBVERSION

Top Gun: Maverick saved the movie theater. It was the biggest domestic box office success of the year. Crowds wept and returned to the theaters for repeated viewings. Critics, who had long since given up expecting sincerity from a summer blockbuster, wrote reviews that felt like love letters. People said things like, "This is what movies used to feel like."

On the surface, *Top Gun: Maverick* might have seemed like a rehash of the Modern Story, but upon closer examination, there were signs that this film was tapping into the metamodern vibe shift. One of the clearest signs of this was how *Top Gun: Maverick* inverted our expectations for subversion. They didn't give Maverick the Luke Skywalker treatment from *The Last Jedi*. There was no unmasking of the Navy as a propaganda machine or any effort to turn the heroic into a subversive eye roll. Subversion had become a trope, but *Top Gun: Maverick* inverted our expectations for subversion, giving us post-ironic fighter jets, fist bumps, and aspirational heroism once again.

It wasn't a naive sincerity either. It was the kind of self-aware *embracing the cringe* that made the Creed comeback work. While there wasn't any Deadpool-esque breaking of the fourth wall, you got the sense that everyone knew they were in a *Top Gun* sequel, but without using any of the ironic detachment techniques we were used to. The infamous beach volleyball scene from the original is replaced with a beach football scene. Maverick buzzes the tower, and John Hamm's character gives a subtle "not this again" grimace. It was a self-aware re-remembering of our dismembered past that made us ache for some of the best values we had lost.

But it wasn't just a re-remembering of the values we lost; *Top Gun: Maverick* also subtly synthesized contributions from the postmodern critique in ways that dropped all the typical subversive preachiness. The 1986 original was overwhelmingly white and male. It reflected the cultural and cinematic norms of the time. *Top Gun* had all the bro energy of a protein shake mixed with shirtless, beach volleyball sweat and Cold War testosterone. *Maverick* didn't throw out that bro energy, but it also didn't dismiss some of the more valid postmodern critiques—especially the concerns that the modern meritocracy didn't allow certain types of people to play the game under the same rules as those who looked like Tom Cruise.

Top Gun: Maverick brought in a new generation of pilots who were more diverse in gender and race than the original. Yet, it didn't do this in a way that framed success for those the postmodernists like Foucault had dubbed as "marginalized" as being the result of a ruthless zero-sum game determined by the will for power. Phoenix was a female fighter pilot who wasn't anyone's love interest, unlike all the women in the original *Top Gun*. She's a serious, respected peer in the squad who's earned her stripes, and yet we don't get moralizing lectures about how the patriarchy has stood in her way, nor do we get her success pitted up against Maverick or Rooster as if she could only be successful through the demotion of men.

Fanboy and Payback are competent pilots of color who are represented in ways that we didn't see in the original *Top Gun*, and yet we don't get any moralizing lectures on how the original movie got it wrong. There are no long expositions from any character that sound anything like, "You know what's wrong with the old Top Gun?" The movie doesn't mock the old guard. There are no lengthy expositions about diversity and representation, even though the cast is more diverse than the original *Top Gun*.

There's not an ounce of deconstruction in *Top Gun: Maverick* either. It seamlessly synthesized those postmodern critiques into a positive vision for reconstruction, embraced the cringe, and made you tear up at the thought that maybe we don't have to discard our old heroes and values. Maverick still goes through a process of learning, growth, and character development, but without any of the cynicism, ironic detachment, and nihilism we became so accustomed to seeing in our cultural stories.

In college, my friends and I would regularly watch *Top Gun*, but it was purely for ironic mockery. I had never wanted a sequel and still didn't think one was necessary when I first saw the trailer. I was braced for cringe, but *Top Gun: Maverick* made me unironically and unexpectedly feel something good. Aspirational. Hopeful. A little less cynical. Maybe even a bit grateful for those slices of Americana that make the country I live in feel like home. Those feelings were needed. The same is true of other unexpected successes with metamodern vibes like the sequel no one asked for in *Twisters* (2024) and a metamodern *Days of Thunder* in Brad Pitt's *F1: The Movie* (2025).

Literally, no one asked for a sequel to the 1996 disaster film *Twister.* The original wasn't exactly high art that moved the zeitgeist needle much. It was fun and made a ton of money, but it wasn't tapping into any of that burgeoning postmodern energy of the '90s that could win you critical acclaim with the intelligentsia. Like Creed's debut release that next year, the original *Twister* was one of those Modern Story holdovers still clinging for dear life to the cultural moment. It was sincere in the most unironic, Spielberg-lite way. Exactly the sort of thing that was dying with Superman.

Fast-forward to 2024, and the creatively titled sequel *Twisters* gave us a wholesome and sincere metamodern inversion of our expectations for subversion. Instead of dodging the cringe and giving us an ironic takedown of the original, it followed the same pattern of *Maverick* and celebrated its past in a self-aware way that was unashamedly post-ironic. *Twisters* was just full-on cringeworthy sincerity.

One of the most disarming surprises in *Twisters* is that it doesn't follow the well-worn script we've come to expect from post–#MeToo Hollywood storytelling: a brilliant, capable female protagonist who has to prove herself by triumphing over the emotional immaturity, ego, or incompetence of the men around her. In the Postmodern Anti-Story, male figures—especially white, rugged ones who signal baseline levels of testosterone—are either comic relief, bumbling relics, or direct antagonists to female growth. It's a narrative reflex that, while sometimes earned and understandable, often ends up flattening the characters into archetypes of resentment and creating a cyclical pattern of zero-sum conflicts between the sexes.

But *Twisters* doesn't go there. It zigzags. It inverts the subversion.

Yes, the central figure is a capable and determined female meteorologist named Kate (played by Daisy Edgar-Jones), who has walked away from the trauma of storm-chasing and must bravely reenter the chaos with more at stake than just meteorological data. But what's unexpected is that she's not surrounded by a cast of fragile men who need to be either conquered or coddled. Enter Glen Powell's character, Tyler: a rugged, charismatic thrill seeker leading a group of internet-famous weather cowboys who seem, at first, like they've stepped out of the cliché handbook. Brace yourself for another lecture about toxic masculinity, right?

Wrong. Instead, we get a zigzag. An inversion of the subversion trope. Tyler has a high-testosterone, braggadocious approach to storm tracking, but when a tornado ravages an Oklahoma town, he applies that confident strength and leadership to mobilizing clean-up efforts, distributing supplies, and rebuilding the community from the rubble.

Instead of a story where Tyler is shown up as a fool or cast as a domineering, misogynistic oppressor of women, what we get is a story where Kate's inherent femininity, with its own set of strengths, balances Tyler's instinctual boldness and helps direct it toward its highest potential. Simultaneously, Tyler's masculinity doesn't overshadow Kate or relegate her to a completely helpless damsel in distress; instead, his boldness in the face of fear and willingness to do what feels dangerous calls Kate to face the fears of her own trauma. He literally drives her into a storm and confidently stays in it with her to show her that she *can* overcome. By the end, what they both have learned from each other is necessary to save the day.

Their dynamic doesn't play into the typical power struggle. It's not about one character outshining the other or proving who has the moral or intellectual high ground. Instead, the film reveals something refreshingly countercultural: Masculinity and femininity aren't enemies in a zero-sum game. It's a vision of co-creation and mutual flourishing, an aspirational longing for Communion.

F1: The Movie, starring Brad Pitt, makes all the same moves. Pitt's character, Sonny Hayes, is a cocky, intense, ambitious race car driver. He's got all the classic masculine energy in the same archetypal mold as Indiana Jones, Michael Jordan, and Tom Cruise's Maverick. Kerry Condon's character, Kate McKenna, is intelligent, poised, and emotionally grounded—a perfect counterbalance to Pitt's Hayes. Like *Twisters*, this film points to a partnership where strength and empathy, ambition and listening, can functionally coexist and increase the virtues of each person's character development in a mutually beneficial way.

Sonny and his rival teammate Joshua both realize, over the course of their character arcs, that meaning in life isn't attached to individual achievement but to the shared flourishing of the group. Human communities are not, at their core, about a struggle for dominance but a shared venture of sacrifice that increases the well-being of all.

As Kate exhorts them both in the final race, in order to win, "Someone has to sacrifice!"[1] These headstrong racers, along with each member of their team, learn that their own good is inextricably linked to the good of their fellow teammate. To win, each must be willing to yield self-centered concerns and sacrifice in love for the good of the other.

These are stories that resonated with audiences because they did more than just present them with something they should be against. They offered a positive vision of what we should aspire toward, grounded in the core conviction that "someone has to sacrifice" for any of this story we share together to work.

THE PURPOSE OF NOSTALGIA

Films like *Top Gun: Maverick*, *Twisters,* and *F1: The Movie* remind us of the ache we'd almost forgotten we had. They utilize nostalgia to invite the audience to retrieve some of what they had lost, while weaving in things we had learned since their predecessors originally took to the big screen. In the Postmodern Anti-Story, longing for the past was either sentimental kitsch or dangerous regression. At worst, it was framed as an act of denial or delusion, a refusal to confront progress or the dark truths of history. The past was the enemy, and true progress was defined as moving in any direction, so long as it was away from the past. *See through* the lies of the past and the traditions you were raised in, and you'll be free to self-author a better life.

To be fair, there is plenty of unhealthy nostalgia that can function as escapism. Nostalgia can become a velvet-gloved form of denial, romanticizing eras that were only golden for a fortunate few or simply never existed in the way we've retold them. But nostalgia, in its deeper and healthier form, isn't escapism. It's a longing to learn from the past so that we can orient our "now" toward a proper future.

If you recall what we learned at the beginning of this book about humans being innate pattern hunters, you may remember that stories are the means by which we capture the patterns we have learned about the world and transmit them to others. The stories that last tend to be the ones we have figured out, through culture-wide trial and error, contain the patterns that lead to life. We keep telling "The Three Little Pigs" story at bedtime because we've gone through centuries of cultural trial and error that proves this pattern of wisdom works. This is what people mean when they say that something has "stood the test of time." This is the value of *tradition*.

Tradition is the attempt to pass on the wisdom that says to the next generation, "Pay attention. This pattern works." It is the effort to collect all the patterns that lead to life and pass them on. And yet, because our continually changing world isn't static, and because our perceptions of what leads to life are not infallible, each generation enters into dialogue with the traditions it's received to stress-test them. Unhealthy nostalgia can deceive us into believing that the world remains static and that it could never be better than the past.

One charitable way of looking at the postmodern shift is to see it as the stress-testing of our traditions and stories, bringing overdue attention to some of the patterns and traditions we were clinging to that weren't actually leading to life. Think of stories where women were reduced to being objects of James Bond-esque status and sexual desire. Deconstructing those modern stories was appropriate because living in that pattern isn't a way that leads to life. But this stress-testing eventually went off the rails because the anti-story was ultimately about tearing all the rails down.

Without a better vision of the way in which we should be oriented, we began to discard the patterns of wisdom from the past and attempted to produce new anti-story archetypes instead, like stories where female heroines took on the typically masculine features of Hercules or another '80s action hero to assert their will to power in a zero-sum game of power dynamics conflict. But does that story contain a pattern that will work? Does it lead to life? And if so, how can we know?

Clay Routledge is one of the world's leading psychologists on the subject of nostalgia. His research found that when people experience a crisis of meaning, they use nostalgia as a stabilizing mechanism in an effort to address their psychological disorientation. In fact, he argues that there are vitally important forms of healthy nostalgia that increase psychological well-being, strengthen relationships, reinforce our sense of identity, and, perhaps most surprisingly, make us more open to the future.[2]

According to Routledge's research, the power of nostalgia lies in its ability to reconnect us to existential meaning when we feel like the plot of our life is unraveling. Nostalgia in this sense isn't just wistful daydreaming about getting a Nintendo on Christmas morning back in the fifth grade. That may be one of the best memories ever. But if you drill down deeper, what is it that makes that memory so sweet? What deeper goodness was there that you long to retain?

It wasn't just the button-mashing and power-ups that created the fond memory. It was the sense of belonging. It was the smell of pine needles and cinnamon rolls. It was the realization that someone knew you well enough to give you exactly what you'd been hoping for. That feeling—that you were seen, that you mattered, that your story was being written in the context of family, home, and a narrative with rituals and rhythms—is what you might call "feeling *wholesome*." And wholesome is something you can rebuild upon.

WHOLESOME IS THE NEW CYNICISM

Wholesome is the feeling that what was once fragmented and fractured has been brought back together and reintegrated. It is the sense in our soul of feeling whole, as if there is some deep coherence between our internal story and reality. The ancient Hebrews called it *shalom*—not merely the absence of conflict, but the presence of harmony, right relationship, and flourishing. In the East, the Chinese philosopher Laozi referred to it as the *Dao*, or "the Way," believing that there was a fundamental way that reality worked and that wholeness came from learning to be attuned to that way.

Hebrew prophets and Laozi wouldn't be in full agreement on everything, but we should pay attention to patterns across cultures that share points of harmony. These might signal the existence of a kind of reference note for reality that we should all tune our hearts to. You might think of this as a Pattern of all patterns—a direction that all these stories point to, which can bring us into wholeness.

Healthy nostalgia is a map. Using it well helps us to retrieve a sense of direction. It helps us to recognize that we were going somewhere once, and at the time, it was good. If we can name the goodness that made us feel whole, maybe it can give us a direction to aim for. Nostalgia can reorient us toward a better future by helping us name what it was that made us feel wholesome and by teaching us to listen for that reference note. We might call this having a sense of *resonance*.

Resonance is what tells us, even before our minds catch up, "This matters." It's why the music swells in your chest when Maverick pushes past the demons of his past to sacrificially and aspirationally lead his young Top Gun team, or when Tyler's masculinity and Kate's femininity complement each other in such a way that it leads to the flourishing of their fictional world in *Twisters*. It's why you feel that strange mixture of goose bumps and tears when you hear an old hymn your grandmother used to sing around the house. It's why the story of sacrifice moves us, even if we've seen it a thousand times in everything from Baymax, the puffy white robot in *Big Hero 6*, to Iron Man in *Avengers: Endgame*. Nostalgia points to a deeper pattern that we just can't seem to get rid of. Maybe it's a pattern that humans didn't even create but rather *discovered* as if it were eternally true.

What we have begun to sense in this shift is a culture-wide search for resonance, where re-exploring tradition and the stories of the past seems to hold the key to finding the Pattern of all patterns and rebuilding a life where all parts of our own story can be reintegrated into the one story capable of holding it all together.

DOUBTING THOMAS'S JOURNEY OF RECONSTRUCTION

A young man I know experienced his own story of going through a painful unraveling and an eventual reconstruction. I first met "Thomas" over dinner in the fall of 2021. He had been a devoted Christian in his late teenage years and felt the call to enter Christian ministry, so he enrolled in a nondenominational ministry program. Thomas had a heart full of sincerity and a hope that he could make a difference in the world.

Not long into the program, his sincerity slowly began turning into cynicism as he endured cycles of abuse and mistreatment from spiritual leaders he trusted as guides. It wasn't just Thomas either. Many other young people who wanted to change the world for good and believed they were surrendering their lives to God felt that they, too, were on the receiving end of painful mistreatment. The Superman figures in their life were starting to look like Homelanders.

When Thomas returned home from the ministry program, the pain he had endured became a new lens through which he began to interpret the world and the guiding story to which he had given his life. This story felt increasingly incoherent. When we met together back in 2021, Thomas had a lot of questions about God, the Bible, and the flaws he was beginning to notice in churches everywhere. The doubts he expressed weren't concerning to me. I could see he was in the process of stress-testing the story and traditions he had been living in, and ignoring those challenges wouldn't be healthy.

We had one more meeting later that fall to process more questions together and discuss what this might mean for his marriage, as he had become engaged to a girl who was experiencing similar dissonance with their guiding story. I could tell he had a sledgehammer in hand, but with what he had gone through, there were plenty of things that deserved to be deconstructed.

We lost touch for a few years, and then in the late winter of 2025, Thomas reached back out to me and asked if we could meet again. In the time that had passed since we'd last met, he and his wife had gone through a complete and total experience of domicide. Thomas had taken a sledgehammer to all the walls of faith that had once made up his home. He had detached from his former community of Christian friends and painfully severed ties with people who had once been his closest companions.

He and his wife had stopped attending church, but they still got together with some friends who had gone through a similar deconstruction. Whenever they got together, he found the group coalescing around their pain and cynicism. Eventually he began to notice how sick in his soul he felt after those get-togethers, as if whatever had been fractured in him was splintering into a million more pieces. His sense of loneliness and isolation was increasing, and his meaning crisis was only getting worse.

On top of all this, Thomas's wife had come down with a debilitating mystery illness that eluded all doctors. Her body was breaking down, and no one could pinpoint why. Some days, Thomas would literally have to carry her from place to place as the pain and weakness sapped all strength from her body. Even if Thomas had never endured the psychological and spiritual abuse in the ministry program that began his deconstruction, experiencing this kind of suffering would be more than enough to make someone give up all hope.

As he began to share this story with me, I thought I could see where it was headed. It was a story I had seen too many times throughout the 2010s and into the early 2020s—a young person who is raised in some version of the Christian story gets pulled through church abuse, pain, or unanswered questions into the orbit of the anti-story only to descend into full-blown nihilism or hedonism. But here came the inversion . . .

Thomas found that in the lowest pit of despair, when everything felt like it was collapsing around him, maybe that old practice of prayer couldn't do any harm. Maybe crying out to the God he didn't believe in anymore could at least make him feel better than the pain of this infinite fragmentation of his soul.

He had become the antihero who had acquired the seeming superpower of *seeing through* it all, but staring into the void, he realized he had nothing to see. The darkness was overwhelming—and far worse than the old house of faith he'd once lived in. So he began to look back through his past, not with a sledgehammer, but with a metal detector to search for whatever gold he may have hastily left behind in the rubble.

Even the simple cry to a God he wasn't sure he believed in felt better than sitting in that circle of cynical friends tearing the world down. It wasn't like a sudden miraculous beam of light filled Thomas's room, but stepping back into that simple practice of prayer was like a ping that went off on his metal detector. It felt *wholesome.* This was a sign that some gold could be retrieved from the rubble. What else could be found that could make him feel just a little bit more whole?

Searching for *something to see* became a completely different exercise for Thomas from all the looking back he'd done in his deconstruction in order to *see through.* The more he looked for the good that gave him that sense of wholeness, the more he realized that mingled with all that was broken was also all of this beauty he had forgotten. Over and over, he saw more and more signs: There was so much in the guiding stories of his past that didn't need to be discarded but rather *built upon.* The sense of fragmentation was decreasing. He was reintegrating his story.

Even his wife's body slowly began to heal. Doctors finally started to see what was broken, and a pathway toward restoration became clear. Thomas's ability to look back and find the places of resonance where that metal detector of reconstruction started pinging for signs of gold reminded him that church wasn't all bad either. There were wholesome memories there, too, which were so much better than the cynical prison he had found himself trapped in. He and his wife both began to wonder, "What if we tried going to church again?"

From that moment on, Thomas began the process of a reconstruction that was even more rapid than his deconstruction. As he sat across from me on that day, nearly four years removed from when he began to be pulled into the anti-story, he was a changed man. He and his wife had restored broken relationships and found community in a new church with people who were on a similar trajectory of positive reconstruction within a more holistic and time-tested Christian story. Thomas had also found a new profession as a clinical therapist who helped others who had their own experiences of fragmentation find wholeness inside a better story. As strange as this may sound, he even looked physically healthier and wiser, as if Gandalf the Grey had become Gandalf the White after being resurrected from the dead.

THE STORY OF STORIES AND THE PATTERN OF PATTERNS

What Thomas went through—the painful unraveling of his old story, the ache of spiritual homelessness, the disillusionment with heroes, the slow rediscovery of what was still good and true—is not just his story. It is *our* story. It is the symbolic journey our entire culture has begun stumbling through.

Thomas didn't find his way forward by denying the dissonance he experienced and doubling down into a close-minded fundamentalism, nor did he find his way forward by self-authoring a new story from scratch. Not only did he scan the rubble of his own past for hints of gold—he also began to look across time and culture for the patterns of wisdom that seemed to have stood the test of time and produced more of the wholesome. In his study of theology and philosophy, he found that the true, the good, and the beautiful seemed to have a common thread, as if there were some transcendent pattern from which all true patterns derive their trueness.

A Story that holds all true stories, if you will.

The ancients called this idea "the music of the spheres."[3] They believed that the planets, the stars, and the heavens weren't just randomly scattered across a cold, indifferent void. They moved according to a divine order, a choreography so precise and beautiful that, if our ears were properly attuned, we would hear it not as noise but as music. The "music" goes unseen, organizing beauty that undergirds all existence.

It was a way of saying that there is a *Way* things are meant to fit. There is a wholeness underneath the surface of all the fragmentation we feel. It draws us to union. To connection. To communion. The wholesome is fundamental. Goodness—not malevolent power, pain, or brokenness—is where the story of reality begins.

This ancient intuition—that the world hums with a Pattern of patterns—is exactly what our experience of resonance points toward.

When Maverick's and Rooster's sacrificial acts of love, set to soaring guitar solos, make your heart unironically pound a little stronger . . .

When you watch the masculine and feminine lay down their zero-sum contest for power at a Tuesday afternoon matinee and something unexpectedly stirs within you . . .

When singing along to a guileless power ballad at a baseball stadium moves you to drop your pretentious detachment to anything too sincere . . .

When you find yourself weeping as you sit in a musty old pew while a lady with white hair plods along on an organ to an uncool three-hundred-year-old song that has you singing, "Tune my heart to sing thy grace . . ."

That's more than nostalgia. It's the tuning fork of your soul vibrating in recognition of the deeper symphony underneath all things. It's how you, me, Thomas, and countless others are finding the Way again.

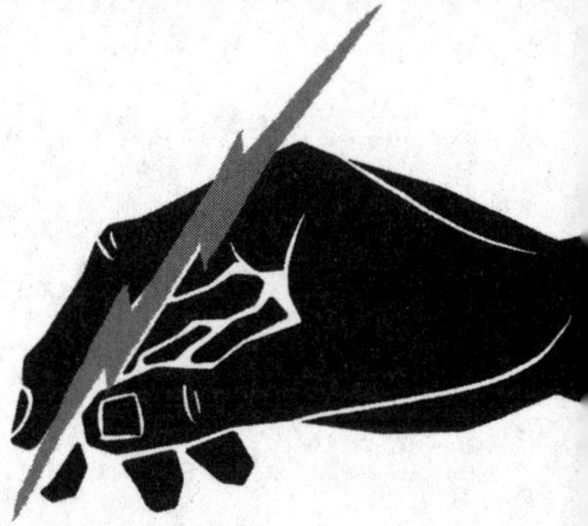

CHAPTER 9

Can a Little Country Church Save the World?

> We shall not cease from exploration
> And the end of all our exploring
> Will be to arrive where we started
> And know the place for the first time.
>
> *T. S. Eliot*

Jordan Hall might be one of the most brilliant people I've ever met. If I had to guess, I would say he's probably in the over-160-IQ club. Hall made millions pioneering world-changing tech startups and then turned his attention to saving the world. Literally.

But the solution he found to civilizational collapse wasn't where he'd expected it.

Ever since he was a kid, Hall could pick up on patterns better than most. Being a polymath has largely gone out of fashion with the Leibnizes of the world, but Hall is just one of those rare breeds. After changing the internet with the development of the MP3 file and digital online video as the CEO of DivX, Hall realized that the Modern Story's promise of perpetual technological progress leading to a techno-utopia of pure reason was a lie. The future of Western civilization was far more likely to be on the path to *Mad Max* than *Star Trek*. It wasn't that we had a problem with just one system—we had a fundamental problem in civilization's underlying code.

So Hall began partnering with some of the leading thinkers in the world who were at the cutting edge of science, technology, philosophy, and anthropology to map the pattern of why civilizations rise and fall. We're not talking a collection of random Reddit posters here, but Nobel Prize–winning scientists, Ivy League PhD mathematicians, and Silicon Valley's brightest and best. As they mapped out what had led to the rise and fall of past human civilizations, they noticed something deeply alarming about our current moment: We were in a *metacrisis*. Ecological, political, economic, and spiritual—all interconnected crises were beginning to unfold simultaneously.

As if it couldn't get any worse, we had a fundamental problem with the way we even solve problems. Like a game of existential Whac-a-Mole, one proposed solution seems to only create another problem. When global markets are headed for catastrophe, leaders attempt to financially stabilize the markets with short-term plans that only seem to create worse long-term problems, passing on more burdensome debts to future generations. At grocery stores in the '90s, we were encouraged to use plastic bags instead of paper bags to save the trees, but we ended up polluting our oceans with plastic and poisoning our bodies with microplastics as a result. We created social media to share family pictures with old friends from college and unintentionally built networks that increased political polarization, teenage anxiety, and doomscrolling-related depression. Maybe there's a problem with our underlying civilizational code.

Hall and others investigating our metacrisis called this game of civilizational Whac-a-Mole "Game A" and concluded that if we're going to avoid a Mad Max future, we'd have to play a different game entirely. So Hall started exploring something called "Game B." He realized that to avoid hell on earth, humanity would have to move away from this game we had been playing and consider a fundamentally different game.

Game A runs like a carnival game rigged to keep you playing even after the prizes have lost their shine. It's a system designed for short-term success: Grab as much power as possible, sell the most dopamine hits, and survive the next quarter. But beneath the flashing lights and clattering machinery, the system is devouring itself and creating new problems faster than it can solve the old ones. Game B was the name they gave to a different dream. A civilization that wouldn't just grow but would heal. Wouldn't just survive but would make wholeness the point again. It wouldn't be built by taking the old schematics and tweaking them. It would emerge where people lived together in right relationship to one another, to the land, to the truth. It would sound, if you had ears to hear, less like the shriek of empires marching in all their technological might to visions of unfettered progress and more like the music of the spheres.

Jordan Hall was looking for the *wholesome.*

He traveled the world and met with the best and the brightest to figure out what could possibly change us at a code level. While living in Encinitas, California—which, on the surface, had every appearance of being one of the world's most beautiful and coveted places to live—he noticed a disturbing pattern. At the end of every weekend, trash littered the streets. Many who had come in for the weekend didn't care enough about the place to even pick up after themselves. When Hall would go to Silicon Valley, the capital of the Modern Story's dream for a *Star Trek* kind of future that could give humanity a God-less salvation in the stars, he would notice that just on the borders of this supposed tech promised land, the streets of San Francisco were littered with trash, human feces, and used drug paraphernalia.

"This is actually the upside-down world. This is wrongness maximally trying to simulate rightness," Hall explained to me in a one-on-one conversation. The rightness he found came in the most unexpected of places: Black Mountain, North Carolina.

Knowing that what he was looking for in Game B couldn't be found in the Babylons of the world, he and his wife went looking to build a garden. In Black Mountain, they found a quaint little spot devoid of all the gleaming self-actualization of the California coastlines. The first thing he noticed was that he felt like he was going from digital back to analog.

"I go, wow, there are extended families that are multigenerational, that all seem to care for each other and like being in each other's company and can hang together. And there are groups of people that can take care of their community and take care of their world . . . this seems very superficial, but I don't know if you've noticed in modernity—it's very rare. Catastrophically rare."[1]

Hall was noticing that something akin to the Game B he had been looking for was already present here. There wasn't a lot of material wealth in Black Mountain, but the people were connected—and they picked up each other's trash purely out of the desire to do what was right for their neighbor. What Hall told me next started to bring it all together. He described the town as "really wholesome."

Wholesomeness is interesting because *wholesome* has to do with wholes, not parts. You don't get these hypersalient spikes—like, "Wow, that's an incredibly beautiful house surrounded by terribly sad people and drug addicts." Everything kind of hangs together.

HOLDING IT ALL TOGETHER

But what was holding it together? What was producing this resonance with the wholesome? Why was Hall hearing the music of the spheres in this little town of Black Mountain, North Carolina?

It wasn't long after finding a home there that Hall and his wife were invited to a two-year-old's birthday party. A gathering of strangers in a small town, where he and his wife had just moved, wasn't exactly the meeting of Nobel Prize winners and Silicon Valley tech gurus he was accustomed to. At the party, someone extended an innocent invitation to Hall and his wife: "Would you like to come to church with us sometime?"

The invitation wasn't a blinding Paul-on-the-road-to-Damascus kind of epiphany. It landed on Hall like an invitation to go get ice cream.

It resonated with him positively, like it was just another slight beckoning of the wholesome. Funny enough, his wife just the day before had the strangest of inclinations hit her: "I think we should be going to church." Church was something that, in all their pursuits for a new way of life that could actually lead to life, had never come up until now.

Hall knew the Game A, Whac-a-Mole thing wasn't working, but confessed, "I didn't really know anymore how things work, but I definitely knew that things were going well here. And if that's the invitation this place has given us, I'm going down that path."

On the Sunday they were planning to attend church, Hall had already been booked to take part in a San Francisco AI conference, so his wife popped into the little country church instead. She reported back and asked Hall, "What do you think about the pastor coming to talk to us about Jesus?" Hall instantly corrected himself as he shared his story with me: "Actually I think she said 'God' at the time; we weren't saying Jesus yet. Jesus was still too far." Once again, a sense of resonance with the wholesome made him feel like this might be worth exploring. Six weeks later, they were attending church every Sunday and Wednesday, and Hall began to notice something. All of the things he was looking for in Game B were happening in this no-name country church. "Remember that big list of 'what does it need to look like?' What does a minimum viable place look like that can actually simultaneously navigate the crisis and possibly be the foundation from which we can respond to the crisis? I'm noticing all the boxes are being checked."[2]

Everywhere Hall looked in this humble Christian community, he saw the civilizational code he had been looking for. On some level, it was absolutely absurd. Is this that God choosing the weak things—the foolish things—again? "They're all showing up in each other's lives and they all focus simultaneously at the highest of the possible high and in the most basic foundational low." Hall saw that average, everyday people in this little church were united around a shared story that directed their gaze upward toward what should be of ultimate concern, and yet this story also gave a directional telos to even the most mundane activities of their daily lives. It was the music of the spheres—all that was seemingly fragmented being held together in unity.

Hall continued to reflect: "I'm drinking it in. The part of me that is not all in the intellectual mode is going, 'This is good. It's not just good—it's Goodness itself. I want more of this.'" But the resonance in his soul that was making him feel whole was moving quicker than his genius-level IQ brain could piece together:

> So then what happens is my mind, is like I sit down and my mind is over here in this chair, and my soul's over in this chair. My soul's like, "I want to keep going to church." My mind says, "Yeah, but you don't actually *believe* what they're saying." And that feels kind of rude. Like you can't keep drinking their water if you actually don't believe with them.
>
> So my soul goes to my mind and says, "All right, dude, it's on you. Work on it. What do you got? Come back to me. If you can demonstrate that this is actually ultimately a bad idea, then we're out. But if not, then full commitment. Go."[3]

So for the next six months, Hall treated his investigation into this story he had found himself already living in like it was another tech startup. He was giving twelve to sixteen hours a day to studying and reading historic Christian theology, philosophy, and the Bible. "I work through it all, and my mind is like, 'Dude. Turns out this thing's real!'"[4]

DISCOVERING THE CENTER OF REALITY

Like C. S. Lewis generations before, Jordan Hall had found the Story from which all true stories derive their trueness. He found the Pattern of all patterns. He saw that at the "center of the totality of reality" was the crucifixion of Christ.[5] Resonance. Wholeness. Reconstruction. The place where immanence and transcendence meet. The culmination of every longing of the Hebrew prophets and the Greek philosophers, and the kernel of truth that continues to last in all of the stories in every culture that stands the test of time.

Hall boldly announced, "It's how the whole thing hangs together." Once he realized this story could integrate it all and change not just the tactics that keep our Whac-a-Mole game going, but could change human nature at the *code* level, his heart and mind made a joint decision. "You can no longer even vaguely not believe all the way down to the core of your being," he told himself. "Well, I guess I'm a Christian then. Better get baptized."

Jordan Hall experienced a conversion in the deepest sense of the term. He realized that the Modern Story's promise of a utopian world didn't have the coherence that could lead to that end. In its latest iterations, the modernist's hope for humanity was to eventually escape this planet, which is destined for destruction, and start the process anew on Mars. This story had no means of addressing the fundamental problem, which was that human nature is bent toward that which does not lead to life. As C. S. Lewis presciently predicted in his Space Trilogy series, taking what is *bent* in our souls to Mars doesn't lead to our salvation. It just brings our propensity for death to Mars.

Our ache for the Transcendent could not be filled by merely increasing our material possessions, expanding our home beyond new continents to new worlds, or building a technological tower of Babel that could elevate us to gods. The pursuit of those things as ends in themselves is a *code-level* problem.

What Jordan Hall learned in a little country church in Black Mountain, North Carolina, was that what we are really searching for to make us whole is *communion*. It dawned on him that there may be something to the postmodern anti-story's suspicion that power might be the name of the game behind Game A. Society does seem to be held together by the threat of force. Even here in Minneapolis, after George Floyd and the subsequent riots that burned much of our city, even the perception that the police may be defunded created a historic spike in violent crime.

You'd like to think that even without the threat of force, people would not want to kill their neighbors or carjack them, but when there isn't anything more than the threat of force to hold people together, our major cities—the very hubs of civilization—unravel into increased violence and crime.

Hall would be the first to admit that his little country church isn't free from all problems, and Black Mountain isn't the perfect utopia. But power and the threat of force don't keep people from killing each other in the pews. Communion does. Communion between the transcendent God and each person, as well as communion between people, is the cosmic glue that holds it all together. Communion is the foundation of healthy community, and community is the foundation of a healthy society.

Hollow out the core of communion, and it all starts to collapse—community, society, and civilization. Nietzsche was right to worry that the death of God in the West would lead to a destabilizing crisis of meaning, but Nietzsche misunderstood God. He associated God with power, so naturally, if power and the threat of force are what hold it all together, then in the vacuum of power left by the death of God, all we would be left with is the zero-sum game for power. The fears of the postmodernists are valid.

MADE FOR COMMUNION

But what Hall and millions of others are waking up to in this zeitgeist shift is that something far more wholesome holds it all together. It is an insight so revolutionary, yet so seemingly foolish, that it might lead you to truly see for the first time that praying grandmas in old church basements might have more *true* power than Silicon Valley or Washington, DC. It's an idea found in the theology of John the Beloved—the disciple of Christ who may have been his closest friend—and his protégé.

> God is love . . . No one has ever seen God; but if we love one another, God lives in us and his love is made complete in us. . . .

> God is love. Whoever lives in love lives in God, and God in them. This is how love is made complete among us so that we will have confidence on the day of judgment: In this world we are like Jesus. There is no fear in love. But perfect love drives out fear, because fear has to do with punishment. The one who fears is not made perfect in love. We love because he first loved us.[6]

This is a code-level reordering of our reality. Love, not fear-wielding power, is the engine of creation itself. Communion holds it all together. All of it. Stars in the galaxies far, far away, which we dream of as teeming with life. The loving toil of a farmer in his field, bringing out of the ground the donation of life it has given up for our good. The kiss that follows the vows of a bride and groom, ready to go to the end of the world for each other. The casserole an old widow at the church brings to the potluck in the church's fellowship hall.

All of it held together by Communion.

Within this Story of stories, Communion names the presence of right relationship with God (that which is necessarily of ultimate concern), with others, with ourselves, and with creation. In Latin, *communio* means something akin to "shared participation" or "oneness together." In this Story, the claim that "God is love" isn't just some sentimental nicety you can plaster on Precious Moments figurines. It's naming a cosmic, metaphysical reality that *all of this* was born from love. It's what John Mark McMillan and his wife, Sarah, wrote together in their song "Born from Love" after their rediscovery of this Communion pulled them out of the anti-story's orbit:

> I was born from Love
> And into Love I'll go
> When I leave the stream behind
> The River I will know
> I was born from Goodness
> In Goodness I will go
> Light to light

And Love to Love I'll go
All my, all my rivers run
All my rivers are running back to You.[7]

The ache for the wholesome is a coded memory of the Communion we were made for. If you look around at our culture over these last few years, you'll start to notice that ache everywhere. Soon you won't be able to unsee it. It's why a Ted Lasso or a new Superman, whose sincerity and wholesomeness in a world that is still stuck in cynicism, resonates with so many. It's why entire TikTok and YouTube trends of "Cottagecore"—which features videos of people baking bread, tending gardens, sewing and crocheting, and slowing down the pace of life—resonate. It's why a bespectacled, cardigan-wearing, method actor and comedian named Joe Pera became a cult hero in the critically acclaimed *Joe Pera Talks with You*. Joe wins the audience's heart not by being edgy or loud, but by gently narrating the beauty of beans, breakfast, and why it's a blessing to have an extra fridge in your garage if you live in the Midwest.

Everything Everywhere All at Once telling us to trade in our nihilistic everything bagels for a dose of sincerity. Deadpool's longings for Christ. *Top Gun: Maverick* and Creed taking you higher. All of it a yearning for the wholesome, a yearning for connection—a yearning for Communion.

From Cottagecore to Creed concerts, these cultural signposts expose not only our ache for meaningful connection across the horizontal axis with others, but vertical connection with that which is of ultimate concern—God.

The signposts are real, but they cannot be an end unto themselves.

Like Jordan Hall's own journey, the *vibes* must connect us to the transcendent source of all true, good, and beautiful vibes—or they, too, will rot into another illusion of meaning.

But when both the Modern Story and the Postmodern Anti-Story have shaped us to be suspicious of the Transcendent, what can we do? If Love holds it all together, then maybe we can trust that enchantment might pursue us. Maybe we'll be haunted back into the Holy.

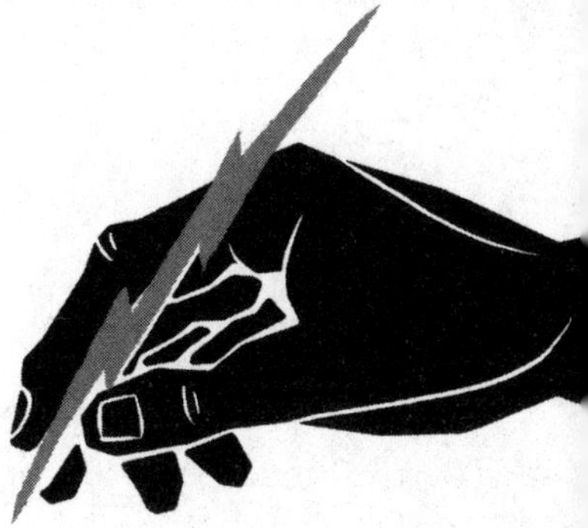

CHAPTER 10

Haunted by Magic

> The serious magical endeavour and the serious scientific endeavour are twins: one was sickly and died, the other strong and throve. But they were twins. They were born of the same impulse.
>
> *C. S. Lewis*

The world is dying.

The light dims, not with the explosion of warheads but with a slow suffocation. Dust sits like a heavy blanket across dying cornfields, faded photographs, and an old farmhouse. It's a slow-rolling apocalypse that runs in the background, like a malaise that the world has learned to live with. Crops are failing, governments are powerless, and history itself is being rewritten to console the children who will inherit nothing, even if the world lasts long enough to allow them to grow old. It's every bit the metacrisis Jordan Hall was worried about but without all the bang and pyrotechnics of a *Mad Max* dystopia. The blight of this end-times scenario feels far more bland and yet far more within reach.

There we meet Cooper, a former NASA pilot turned reluctant farmer who is saddled with the grief of losing his wife to a cancer that the failing Game A world could not heal. He has learned to silence the yearning he once felt for something beyond the closed horizon of a world believed to be nothing more than a slowly decaying planet made up of particles, matter, laws of physics, and survival instincts. Cooper's despair has all but stripped him of his will to search for meaning beyond the immanent. He longs for the past—a past where he felt a sense of meaning and purpose, a past where people were encouraged to "look to the stars for answers."

Running in the background of Cooper's own narrative identity is a story, one that has seemed to run silently beneath the assumptions of both the Modern Story and the Postmodern Anti-Story. Cooper is a man of our time and age—our *secular age,* as philosopher Charles Taylor would call it.[1] He lives with the quiet but constant insistence that whatever we can see, touch, measure, or technologically manipulate is the full extent of reality. The universe is a closed system with no windows to the Transcendent. No God or gods. No spirits or magic. Nothing is sacred in this world. It's all just a show about nothing.

But pressing through the seemingly impenetrable walls of this closed universe comes a haunting apparition. A ghost in his daughter's bedroom, which he desperately wants to explain away but can't, disrupts his grasp of reality. This ghost in his daughter's bookshelf becomes the white rabbit he chases into the beyond, into a disorienting wonderland among the stars. This journey slowly nudges him away from a story closed to transcendence into a posture of openness toward the possibility of a new story that can hold his repressed aspirations for beauty, love, meaning, and hope.

Few films in the twenty-first century have so hauntingly captured our restless yearning for something beyond the closed horizon of the immanent frame quite like Christopher Nolan's *Interstellar.* As one of the great filmmakers of our secular age, all of Nolan's previous movies fit squarely within the confines of our disenchanted worldview. What pre-enlightened people would have seen as magic was just technological sleight of hand that science could not yet explain (see his 2006 film, *The Prestige*). The world of dreams is not a mysterious channel of spiritual communication, as the ancients and those less enlightened in non-Western cultures believe, but rather a strange, computer-like program that runs repressed and painful Freudian memories, which we could theoretically hack with the right technology (as in the 2010 film *Inception*).

Even Nolan's beloved Batman trilogy strips the entire mythological world, filled with its magic, gods, and spiritual superpowers, and converts the strange, liminal world of Gotham into a grounded parody of Chicago or New York City, where nothing transcends scientific explanation. The deepest struggle throughout all of these films is the meaning crisis we feel in our disenchanted world. Whether it's Gotham City or the blight-struck world we encounter in *Interstellar*, these settings serve as placeholders for our experience of living in a closed universe devoid of any higher source of meaning beyond matter in mindless motion. What could salvation possibly look like in such an absurd universe?

In *Interstellar*, Cooper's movement from apathy to aspiration begins as he finally comes to believe that his daughter Murph may not just be having childish fantasies of the supernatural appearing in her bedroom. That constant and yet nearly imperceivable cloud of dust, that symbolic weight of despair—what Charles Taylor called a general *malaise* that saturates everyone and everything in our secular age—takes the shape of a powerful dust storm that blows into the open window of Murph's bedroom. The dust that settles on the floor discloses a pattern that leaves no room for denial. Something more than mindless matter in motion is at work.

This ghostly white rabbit leads Cooper back to his sense of calling as a NASA pilot, commissioned to participate in an interstellar adventure to relocate humanity off this planet, which is doomed for destruction, and find salvation in the stars. It's the Game A plan of salvation that has animated the imaginations of people like Gene Roddenberry, creator of *Star Trek,* and Elon Musk, who dreams of colonizing Mars.

On this voyage beyond our solar system, we meet another sojourner feeling the cross-pressuring of our secular age. Her name is Dr. Amelia Brand. In the language of Charles Taylor, cross-pressuring refers to the psychological and cultural pressure we experience when we're caught between the pull of faith and the push of perpetual doubt. It's a kind of restless middle that we all feel, regardless of whether we have gone to church our entire lives or we're self-proclaimed atheists. To quote James K. A. Smith, cross-pressuring is the feeling "where believers are beset by doubt and doubters, every once in a while, find themselves tempted by belief."[2] Dr. Brand feels a pressure to adhere to the culturally established stories of a closed, material-only universe on one side, while simultaneously feeling a deep sense of its inadequacy on the other. While hurling through the vast void of space, she begins to wonder if *love* somehow transcends.

DOES LOVE TRANSCEND?

Dr. Brand and Cooper grapple over whether or not what we call *love* is merely a biological phenomenon useful in the evolution of our species. We might feel something transcendent attached to it, but in this disenchanted worldview, love is just an evolutionary illusion embedded in our brains to get us to procreate and protect our progeny. Love has no transcendent quality or source. It is just another random feature of a mindless world that keeps this chaotic game of survival continuing. Since Nietzsche's death of God, this has been the story running beneath the modern and postmodern currents.

Dr. Brand is increasingly haunted by the possibility that love may be "one thing we're capable of perceiving that transcends the dimensions of space and time."[3] Her lover was sent out on an earlier mission to search for a habitable world, and she now has a feeling in her gut that his planet could be the one setting that could save humanity. Cooper feels a *resonance* with the Transcendent in his love for his children, but his head remains situated in the disenchanted secular story.

Like Jordan Hall, whose sense of resonance at a little country church made him *act as if* the Transcendent were real before his mind could catch up, or like songwriter John Mark McMillan, whose sense of resonance with the practice of singing old Charismatic worship choruses started changing his story before his rational mind could fully okay the change, Cooper continues to act as if there were some higher meaning to the love he experiences for his children until the cross-pressuring reaches a breaking point.

This breaking point comes as Cooper has a climactic confrontation with the symbolic gatekeeper of our godless, disenchanted, secular story—a character aptly named Dr. Mann. Dr. Mann was part of the prior "Lazarus" missions, a theologically appropriate name for a mission to resurrect humanity from inevitable death, which had stranded him on this icy planet as he searched for habitable worlds. Dr. Mann deceives Cooper and Dr. Brand in an effort to preserve his own life, lying about the fitness of the planet to sustain human life. He also attempts to kill Cooper in order to hijack his ship and escape from the barren world.

In this violent confrontation between Dr. Mann and Cooper, Mann explains to Cooper that the feelings of love Cooper has for his children are not evidence of any transcendent source or meaning. There's nothing sacred behind them. All of our notions of the good, the true, and the beautiful are driven by meaningless evolutionary forces in our biology. The strongest of those forces is our instinct for survival, and if Mann's survival comes at the cost of another's death . . . well, that is simply how natural selection works.

If God is dead, then we are the only authoring agents left in the universe. Good is only what I perceive to be beneficial to my story. But what happens when our radical self-authoring of what is good produces conflicting visions of what is good with others? As internally coherent as Mann's story may appear, it repulses us because deep down we know that a world filled with Dr. Manns—where all we have left is a ruthless contest of wills—does not lead to life. Self-authoring cannot scale. We need a shared story that transcends us, one that can provide a shared moral framework so we can live well together. What happens next in this story resonates with us because it adheres to the Pattern of patterns we perceive across all the stories that stand the test of time.

Cooper's survival of the attack becomes the symbolic death of Dr. Mann's story in Cooper's mind and heart. There, in all the glory of an immersive IMAX screen, accompanied by the sounds of a crescendoing church pipe organ that harkens our attention to the sacred, that Pattern of patterns emerges. Cooper's heroism takes on the shape of the Cross, revealing what the ultimate form of love looks like.

When it seems that all hope may be lost, Cooper rejects his own evolutionary instinct for self-preservation and sacrifices his life so that Dr. Brand and the rest of humanity on Earth might live. The only hope for humanity is his descent into the belly of a black hole. It's a cosmic sign of Jonah.

But Cooper is not abandoned unto death as he descends into this abyss. Instead, he emerges on the other side of the void transformed. His heart and his head come into alignment with a singular epiphany: *Love transcends.* Dr. Brand's earlier intuition that love may be drawing her to the only habitable world that can sustain a rescued humanity proves to be correct. Her decision to follow the pull on her heart and choose that particular world among all other options was not irrational. It was *suprarational.*

The story is among Christopher Nolan's most spiritually resonant, naming the ache for the Transcendent we all feel. It gives voice to our culture's longing to live in a story that can coherently hold how our experiences of resonance with the true, the good, and the beautiful call us upward into Communion with their very transcendent Fount. It hints at the eternal pattern we see in all great stories—we were made from Love, and that Love beckons us to return.

But Nolan's conclusion in the film still comes up short. In the end, we are still alone in the universe, with no one to look out for us but ourselves. Murph's "ghost" was always just her father, Cooper, who had crossed beyond the limitations of space-time to inhabit her bedroom bookshelf. There may still be no real sacred beyond the scope of what science will one day be able to explain. Nolan's ache for the Transcendent, his longing for a better story, comes so close, and yet he still remains cross-pressured in the immanent frame.

SCIENCE AND MAGIC

When *Interstellar* was released in 2014, it seemed as though our secular age might have no end in sight. New Atheism was still pulling people into their Dr. Mann–like worldview. The number of nones claiming to have no religious adherence continued to rise while church pews continued to empty. But by the end of the 2010s, substantial cracks in the immanent frame began to appear throughout our culture. It was like the hauntingly beautiful music of Hans Zimmer's *Interstellar* soundtrack could be heard coming through the other side of our secular-age bookshelf. Like Cooper, if we were to ever open ourselves up to the Transcendent, we would need some kind of scientific validation of our ghosts.

Trapped in the belief that immanence is all there is, could we dare to hope that a God who is love might lovingly beckon us to Communion through our observations of the immanent? Funny enough, that's exactly what happened. It was our scientists, those who had dedicated their lives to studying the patterns we deduce in the immanent material world, who became unexpected prophets of the Transcendent. In a culture stuck within the story of a mindless universe, it might just be a sign of God's peculiar sense of humor to have used scientists of the mind to spur on our culture-wide spiritual shift.

One such scientist of the mind, whom I have mentioned already in this book, is Clay Routledge. His research on the psychology of existential meaning demonstrates that the nones didn't stop longing for the Transcendent; they just started chasing it in different places. Belief in ghosts, angels, astrology, and aliens was surging even as church attendance was declining in the United States. Routledge concludes that humans are fundamentally a spiritual species, not merely wired for survival but for a meaningful sense of connection to a higher power.[4]

Psychologist Jonathan Haidt demonstrates that the longing for transcendence doesn't just manifest itself in churches or monasteries, but also in football stadiums, political rallies, and yoga studios. California bourgeois bohemians sitting in a hot yoga studio might not call what they experience there "God." They might call it "the Universe," but what their words are aiming for is a naming of the Transcendent. Haidt argues that the longing to move past self-focused concerns and connect with something beyond ourselves and beyond pure rationality cannot be shut off. A professing atheist, he became increasingly concerned that, with a longing for transcendence seemingly baked into the human condition, we may fall for dangerous pseudo-religions, such as political tribalism, "wokeism," and Silicon Valley utopianism instead.[5]

Iain McGilchrist, a psychiatrist, philosopher, and literary scholar, argues that our disenchanted worldview is the result of a culture that has become dominated by the brain's left-hemisphere analytical and utilitarian modes of thinking. Our cultural incentives, which prioritize this analytical way of engaging with the world, come at the expense of our more intuitive ways of apprehending the world, which is associated with the right hemisphere of the brain.[6]

The tragedy, McGilchrist warns, is not that the left hemisphere is wrong, but that it has become a tyrant, cutting us off from the richer, more integrated perception of the world that the right hemisphere once mediated. It is a way of knowing reality, not just through rationality but through resonance. According to McGilchrist, we have become blind to the sacred not because it isn't there, but because our way of knowing has been flattened, hemmed in by a guiding story that only counts what can be measured, dissected, or controlled. Other ways of knowing have been affirmed by nearly every culture, past and present, outside our narrow sliver of recent Western culture. What makes us believe that we have the whole picture, especially when the result is this crisis of meaning?

McGilchrist argues that our meaning crisis stems from our loss of *noetic knowing,* which tethers us to a sense of the Transcendent. This is the kind of knowing that doesn't come from crunching numbers on a spreadsheet or performing lab tests under a microscope. It doesn't deny what can be learned from those things, but this *knowing* is different. It comes from a sudden clarity, a felt coherence, that sense of resonance with the wholesome, a deep-down recognition that something is true, like it's registering in your soul before your brain can fully analyze it. Analytic knowing says, "That mountain is fourteen thousand feet high." Noetic knowing says, "I've climbed to the summit and wept at the beauty I beheld."[7]

Cognitive scientist John Vervaeke believes that our meaning crisis is not just the result of chemical imbalances in the brain causing unprecedented spikes in depression and suicide. As we've learned in previous chapters, Vervaeke argues that the mental health data points to a culture-wide experience of domicide taking place in our midst. Like McGilchrist, Vervaeke states that our culture had overemphasized *propositional knowing* as the supreme form of knowledge, diminishing the value of other kinds of knowing central to our human experience.[8]

Propositional knowing is like McGilchrist's left-hemisphere, analytical knowing. It is the knowledge of facts and beliefs we collect in the form of propositions, such as "cats are mammals." That proposition tells you something true about cats, but it isn't the same knowing that comes from petting a particular cat or having a cat as a family pet. For Vervaeke, this overemphasis on the propositional denies the other vital kinds of knowing that our brain regularly engages in to make sense of the world and reconnect us to transcendence. These other types of knowing are called (1) Procedural (knowing how to do something), (2) Perspectival (knowing what something is like from a particular vantage point), and (3) Participatory (knowing through being, through embodied, transformative connectedness).

We don't learn how to ride a bike by reading an instruction manual about it. We learn how to ride a bike through the *procedural* steps of getting on a bike, pedaling, and balancing. We know what it's like to ride a bike not from reading a book about it, but from the *perspective* we gain from actually riding a bike. All my efforts to tell you about the pure experience of joy I had as an eleven-year-old boy riding my bike to my friend's house, while feeling the warm summer air on my face and popping a wheelie with a wad of Bubble Tape gum in my mouth, will fall short of the knowledge I have about this experience. This is a *participatory knowing* that can't be reduced to propositions.

The noetic, participatory ways of knowing have been how humans historically have experienced a sense of the Transcendent. While Vervaeke claims no specific religious adherence, he has publicly mourned our severed connection to a sense of the Transcendent and argued that this disconnect is at the core of our meaning crisis. Like Jordan Hall, one of Vervaeke's closest dialogue partners, Vervaeke sees this meaning crisis as being at the heart of a civilizational metacrisis. Staying locked into the story of our secular age is no longer a scientifically or strategically viable option. In other words, we'd better pay attention to the *vibes* or we'll end up going full *Mad Max*– or *Interstellar*-style global blight.[9]

There can be no talk of scientists of the mind swaying the cultural opinion on transcendence without mentioning the most culturally influential psychologist of the past decade—Jordan Peterson. Peterson's name has become a bit of a lightning rod in the culture war, but there can be no denying his significance. Camille Paglia—an atheist, feminist, and iconoclastic academic—praised Peterson in 2017 as "the most important and influential Canadian thinker since Marshall McLuhan."[10] Peterson's quaint Albertan accent, combined with his fatherly admonishments to young men to clean their rooms, wouldn't exactly be the first qualities you'd imagine from someone who turned out to be the tweed-wearing Terminator of New Atheism.

While New Atheists were busy telling us God was a delusion and life was just atoms bouncing into each other, Peterson came along and said, "Not so fast, bucko!" He had the credentials that the intelligentsia and culture-makers were looking for. An academic who had been a professor at Harvard and the University of Toronto, Peterson also had a clinical therapy practice during the height of the "*therapy as salvation*" cultural moment.

Peterson was an early adopter of YouTube, posting his popular classroom lectures on evolutionary psychology and how to use old stories as "maps of meaning." In May 2017, he rented a Toronto theater and announced that he would be giving talks on the concept of God and stories from the Bible. It was a somewhat strange idea. Peterson had no public profession of faith. This clearly wasn't a Billy Graham evangelistic crusade or a Richard Dawkins–style lecture about the foolishness of believing in God and fairies. Peterson had stepped into the public square, an arena dubbed secular and devoid of any and all religious claims, and told people that we dismiss the Transcendent at our own peril.

People packed the theaters to listen to his lectures, and millions more watched on YouTube. In the new media landscape of podcasts and YouTube, Peterson became a rising star. The most influential voice of this new media age was, and still is, Joe Rogan. Rogan was a living example of everything Clay Routledge's research had shown about nones not abandoning their belief in some form of higher power but merely trading their grandparents' Bibles for magic mushrooms and *Ancient Aliens* episodes. The most listened-to voice in the world, known in his early podcasting days for parroting New Atheist talking points and religious conspiracies from Dan Brown novels, was now sitting down with Peterson for three-hour-long conversations about God and the Bible.

Peterson's fascination with biblical stories was unique. He wasn't treating the Bible as inspired Scripture, nor was he taking a typical postmodern approach to deconstructing Bible stories so that people could *see through* them. He was calling people to read them *to see* something, even if he himself didn't know exactly what that was. Repeated efforts to pin down a proclamation of faith from reporters asking the question "Do you believe in God?" were most often met with a seemingly postmodern word-game response: "Depends on what you mean by *believe*." Peterson would usually follow this up with another provocation: "I suppose I *act as if* I believe in God."

OPENING UP

These scientists of the mind made a compelling case that we don't live in a mindless, material machine. Living as if the world were disenchanted runs contrary to our code-level programming and produces in us a crisis of meaning. Openness to the Transcendent is not *irrational*. It is *suprarational*. It's why we don't give our kids spreadsheets but stories when we want to disclose to them the meaning of the world.

We are hardwired to pursue transcendence. With this realization spreading, another seismic shift in culture was underway. By the 2020s, New Atheism as a cultural force was dead.

The vibe was shifting so much that we actually started believing in vibes. Zeitgeist shifts became real to us again because we reopened ourselves to the possibility that there really are *spirits* that move beneath and through the spirit of the age. Ghosts behind the bookshelf wasn't a fringe belief anymore.

Every possible pursuit of a transcendent power that could reenchant our world was now moving into the mainstream, just as that mainstream shifted from cable news and late-night talk shows to social media, podcasts, and YouTube. By 2023, seven in ten Americans described themselves as being spiritual in some way. Forty-five percent claimed to have experienced a sudden feeling of connection with something beyond this world. Even self-described atheists (60 percent) and agnostics (58 percent) claimed to regularly feel a deep sense of spiritual wonder about the universe—rates that were even higher than Catholics (36 percent) and Protestants (45 percent).[11]

Congressional hearings in which US government officials openly profess belief in contact with "non-human intelligences" have become a seemingly annual occurrence, yet they barely make a blip on the 24/7 news radar. *Independence Day*–style alien invasion could happen in New York City, and Gen Z would simply yawn. Your office coworker could tell you about his ayahuasca retreat with a shaman, and you might think to yourself, "At least that's more interesting than listening to him drone on about the latest Richard Dawkins talk he watched on YouTube like he used to do a few years ago." Young women dabbling with Wicca will gladly introduce themselves as witches and eye-roll the inevitable *Monty Python* jokes from Boomers and Gen Xers who still think that reference is culturally relevant.

Was our secular age coming to an end, or was the cross-pressuring just intensifying? Was our world becoming *reenchanted*?

Those Boomers and Gen Xers with their *Monty Python* references will tell you that this stuff has been around for a while, and they're right. Sociologist Max Weber was writing about disenchantment back in 1918. C. S. Lewis's friend and fellow Inkling Owen Barfield was calling for a McGilchrist-and-Vervaeke-style rediscovery of participatory knowing back in 1949. You might have had an aunt out in California who would call Dionne Warwick's Psychic Friends Network hotline to get a tarot card reading after tantric yoga class back in the early '90s, but everyone kind of looked at her as being on the fringe. Not anymore. Our digital age of social media hyperconnectivity and our increasing awareness of our need for transcendence have moved the fringe into the mainstream.

If our previous cultural mood marked by cynicism, deconstruction, suspicion, and disenchantment could be distilled down to one word, it might be *closedness*. And the zeitgeist shift toward sincerity, hope, embracing the cringe, and reenchantment might be distilled down to one word that captures the change in the posture of our hearts, souls, and minds: *openness*.

Those noetic ways of knowing are back on the table. The windows to transcendence have been flung wide open. Yet, we still have a narrative vacuum, and into this vacuum rushes both light and shadow, angels and demons, meaning and pseudo-meaning. Our ache for Communion can lead to counterfeit connections. Divorced from a coherent guiding story that names what the shape of authentic Communion leading to the wholesome flourishing of creation looks like, our longing for transcendence can become hijacked by dark enchantments—those connections with higher powers that are dressed as light but lead to death.

Our reconstruction must be guided by a spiritual compass pointed toward true north. Because in an age of reenchantment, the question is no longer *if* we will believe in something beyond ourselves but *what* we will believe in. A compass oriented merely toward the spiritual will not do. If there is any wisdom to be found in the stories that stand the test of time, it is that they consistently warn us that not every spirit is holy. We need more than just reenchantment. We need *orientation*.

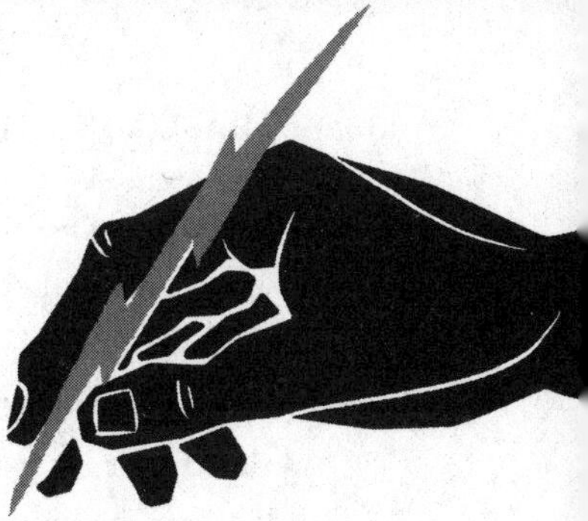

CHAPTER 11

Dark Magic

I'd sold my soul to glut the sensorium, and now
here was my reaper demanding his payment.
Ashley Lande

The ghosts began knocking, not just from behind the bookshelf, but from beyond the bounds of our culturally conditioned worldview. The haunting music of pipe organs and synths called us to explore past the limitations of science and get at the ache that our numbing addiction to screens could not heal. The age of disenchantment was cracking, and a new posture of openness was spreading like wildfire through the zeitgeist. A longing for the wholesome and the sacred, to get us out of this show about nothing, was reshaping our cultural mood.

Ashley Lande is one such sojourner whose life has moved with the rhythm of these zeitgeist shifts. Her life and story have become a sign of the times.

Ashley grew up in a world that was mostly nice and mostly fine, but mostly hollow. It was a polite, disenchanted world filled with Vacation Bible School that taught her to sing "Jesus Loves Me," incentivizing her attendance with snacks and coloring sheets. It was a kind and generally harmless expression of what sociologist Christian Smith calls "moral therapeutic deism"—a type of watered-down spirituality driven by notions of a clockmaker God who winds up the universe, sets it to run on its own, and throws out some general instructions on how to behave nicely and stay out of trouble.[1]

Ashley didn't have a traumatic childhood, just a typical experience of middle America where bushes never burn and mountains are never transfigured, but hey, at least you signed a D.A.R.E. pledge that would keep you from becoming a degenerate, which is something. But Ashley was also raised in the heyday of the anti-story, fomenting a punk rock rebellion toward anything that smelled like the machine, even if that machine had given you delicious fruit snacks after singing "Jesus Loves Me." Sunday school boredom turned into epistemic rebellion in her teenage years. That antihero drive to *see through* all the lies had shaped her soul in a new direction.

Ashley concluded that Christianity wasn't just irrelevant; it was an opiate for people too afraid to rage against the machine. The New Atheist apologist Christopher Hitchens became her new patron saint. That bland, pew-sitting faith, where you'd do some Christian karaoke and listen to a generally less interesting TED Talk from a generally less educated pastor telling you the same lessons about niceness you learned from *VeggieTales* when you were eight, did nothing for the ache in her soul for wonder and to taste the Transcendent. She thought the *seeing through* gave her clarity, but it was really masking despair—a despair Søren Kierkegaard considered one of the worst forms of despair. This is the despair that is unaware it is in despair.[2]

So in her late teen years, Ashley turned to partying, sex, and alcohol to numb her despair. When someone handed her a baggie of dried psychedelic mushrooms in college, it just seemed like a natural progression. She wasn't knowingly taking them for a spiritual experience. It just seemed like she had moved beyond mere booze to the logical next step of being a more mature partygoer with more refined tastes.

As the psilocybin mushrooms gradually worked their way through her system, the colors of Ashley's world slowly became more vivid. The sound waves from the records she was spinning felt more tangible. The boringly beige world she had been living in started to shimmer. She felt a taste of enchantment.

That night opened the windows of transcendence to her, and psychedelics became her new religion. She grew mushrooms with all the care of a priest stewarding the Eucharist. She prayed over her hallucinogens in a scrambled mix of New Age Sanskrit and vibrational intention. This was her new sacrament.

Psychedelic trips were no longer recreational. They were revelatory. Each trip took her on what she felt was an *Interstellar*-like voyage through the cosmos, making her believe that she was glimpsing the secret divine gears that turned the machinery of the universe in motion. And yet, she had no guide. No map. No way to process it all other than to impose whatever meaning her self-authoring story desired.

ENTERING A WORLD OF MAGIC

Ashley had entered a reenchanted world, but one with no distinction between white magic and dark magic. Long before our cultural stories in the West stripped the world of magic and wonder, our time-tested stories had assumed that the world was not only magically but *morally* charged. The cosmos wasn't merely enchanted—it was *contested*. Magic that could heal and magic that could destroy. Merlin versus Morgan le Fay. Fairy godmothers and wicked witches. Moses against Pharaoh's magicians. Gandalf battling Saruman. These are the stories that have stood the test of time because they contain a true pattern of wisdom to be preserved.

Magic always bends toward light or shadow. The question before and beyond the Modern Story was never "Is magic real?" but "Who does this magic serve?" In the secular age, we discarded that wisdom, so when magic reentered the frame, our ache for transcendence and our newfound openness welcomed any and all tastes of higher power.

What Ashley slowly began to realize was that she had fallen into a dark enchantment disguised as light. In her hidden despair and the desperate desire to break through the malaise, she blazed into the beyond without a compass to orient her toward true north. The visions that once sang with beauty began to flicker with oppressive menace. The trips increasingly became terrifying. Ashley kept returning, hoping to recover that early spark of radiance, but what met her instead was panic.

And darkness. Heavy, demonic darkness.

When I first met Ashley in 2022, she told me tales of how demonic apparitions would visibly manifest in her room. This may sound like a relatively common side effect of a bad acid trip, but the problem was that Ashley was completely sober when these unholy ghosts appeared. She wrote of one such experience in her haunting memoir, *The Thing That Would Make Everything Okay Forever*:

> The dark of my room was still now, and my body flooded with dread as I saw it in the corner: a column of black, like a tower of smoke, diaphanous and yet not, substantiating itself as the vapors curled upward and downward and were pulled into a hideous shape approximating a person. "This is not real," I whispered to myself, or rather mouthed, for fear that my declaration would draw some cackling rebuke from the thing. I was paralyzed . . .
>
> Gene [my dog] . . . growled and leaned toward the corner where the thing malingered . . . we were in the presence of evil . . . I'd sold my soul to glut the sensorium, and now here was my reaper demanding his payment.[3]

Ashley was practicing yoga three times a week, had regular meditation sessions with the Buddha statues that adorned her home, and followed every possible white rabbit into any enchanted wonderland she could find. The dull malaise was gone, but a terrifying spiral into the suffocating embrace of some dark sorcerer was her new reality.

She felt like she was dying, but gave her fungal savior, the thing she was convinced would make everything okay forever, one final prayer. She chanted and poured all the positive vibes she could into these homegrown psychedelic mushrooms, stood before the model of a Mayan temple that sat like an altar in her home, and "the Universe cackled malevolently."[4]

Ashley lay down on the floor, certain that this time she would die. She tried repeating all the mantras that had once given her a sense of communion with a power beyond her, but they were powerless to save her from the onslaught of dread. A new realization hit her: "I was alone in a hostile cosmos."[5]

Ashley didn't die on the floor that day. Later, she found her Styrofoam cooler, filled with carefully cultivated mushrooms that had been overtaken by mold, and she felt a strange sense of relief. She didn't want to self-author or self-navigate an enchanted world alone anymore. All the gurus said that the ultimate realization psychedelics would afford was that there was no good and no evil. Such dualisms were illusions of the ego. But she had done everything to get to that place of ego death and beyond, and she now understood, as malevolent apparitions appeared to her in full sobriety, that this supposedly "enlightened" view ran contrary to not only her own experience, but even the most basic observations of a world filled with Hitlers, rapists, and people who send text message scams to the elderly.

Not only did her psychedelic experiences eventually lead her to a deepening state of oppressive darkness, but there was no way for her to live in a shared story with fellow psychonauts around their experiences. Get a hundred people who have taken DMT or mushrooms into a room, and task them with coming up with a shared coherent story that could codify moral instruction to their children, build hospitals and universities, and care for the poor. It has never been done because it *can't* be done.

The Christian story, which had been reduced in her childhood to moral therapeutic deism, slowly began to take on a new light for Ashley. She had become a mother, and in a moment of unexpected, profound awakening—as she felt a sense of love for her children in a world that was clearly filled with brokenness—she started to see. Wonder. Joy. A resonance with the wholesome. In all this love for her children, what direction did she want them oriented toward? It certainly wasn't the path she'd been on. She would never want to give them a Terence McKenna book as a guide for their life. But there was a transcendent pull to this love, and it wasn't being induced by any substance she had ingested. This love was pointing her toward a pattern . . . a *person.*

Ashley became Christ-haunted.

This new holy ghost in her life was drawing her to return to the strangest of places. Not to an on-demand stratospheric launch into cosmic oneness, but to sit in the pews with her husband and children in a simple little church. She experienced neither the bland malaise of her disenchanted youth nor the weighty oppression of the dark enchantments that had disguised themselves as angels of light. She felt something wholesome. A deep white magic that made every bronze Buddha and Mayan temple in her home feel like impotent idols.

Ashley and her husband discarded every ceremonial trinket and every relic of her once-psychedelic religion and submerged themselves in the waters of baptism. The enchantment was still there. The magic was still there. But her allegiance had changed. Ashley found that she now belonged to Someone. Not to the cosmos, not to the Universe, not to the Divine Feminine. She belonged to the One in whom there is no darkness at all.

The words of the hymn she sang in this little brick church—"There is no shadow of turning with Thee"—resonated in the very core of her being. The Holy Ghost had brought her into harmony with the true music of the spheres. The words of the preacher, quoting from the Gospel of John, said, "In him there is light, and there is no darkness at all." And Ashley's heart leaped for joy.

She had found the Story of stories, and with it, the *thing* that would make everything okay forever.

THE FEMININE MEANING CRISIS

Much of the online conversational space around the meaning crisis over the past ten years has been largely driven by male voices deeply concerned about the unique ways in which despair and disillusionment impact young men. All the Andrew Hubermans, David Goggins, and Jordan Petersons of the world attempting to speak to men in a state of despair seem to vastly outnumber their public female counterparts. But Ashley's story reminds us that the meaning crisis and our disenchanted age have a powerful feminine dimension that deserves better understanding.

From a biological and anthropological perspective, women have often demonstrated a more natural capacity for those noetic ways of knowing that Iain McGilchrist advocates for. Some psychologists argue that heightened intuitive abilities may have developed in women to enhance survival and reproductive success in a world where, on average, women tend to possess less physical strength than men. For our ancient ancestors, women who could sense deception, aggression, or erratic behavior from a male suitor could avoid a potential abusive or deceitful mate who might harm her or her children. The women who were more likely to pick up on those cues had a better chance of passing on that ability to their children, who then had a higher chance of survival themselves.

Picking up on those patterns isn't like doing a math problem. It's a subtle, subconscious reading of micro-expressions and body language. It's going to a new area and picking up something that just feels like it's in the wind to warn you: "This place isn't safe." If you ignore that subtle nudge as a strong adult male, you may be able to fend off a human or animal predator in the woods, but if you are a woman with average strength who may have small children with you, ignoring that gut instinct comes with far more risk.

My wife has a notorious track record of being able to read when people we meet are narcissists, morally unstable, or duplicitous. When we were younger, I would argue with her about the lack of evidence for her claims, imposing my left-hemisphere analytical brain on her as the best arbiter of reality. But I've learned, after nearly twenty years of marriage where she has been correct over and over again, to listen to her gut instincts.

This cultivated capacity to pick up on patterns that may be beyond our rational, conscious mental detection systems may be one of the reasons why, across many cultures and eras, women have played unique roles in connecting and discerning the spiritual. Some scientists call this ability *implicit pattern recognition.* You might just call it getting the "ick" when you feel an embodied warning, or picking up on good vibes when there's an embodied sense of safety.

In ancient Greece, you had the *Pythia*, who functioned as the oracle of the god Apollo in Delphi. People traveled from around the world to hear this woman's ecstatic speech. Kings consulted her before battle to discern which way the gods and spirits were moving. Throughout medieval Europe, women commonly functioned as folk healers, using intuitive practices to find spiritual remedies for people's ailments.

While the pursuit of noetic knowing and mystical experience is often framed today through the lens of pagan or alternative spiritualities like the ones Ashley once pursued, the truth is that Christianity also holds a deep, rich tradition of women who practiced and taught a noetic, experiential communion with God. From Hildegard of Bingen (1098–1179) and her cosmic visions, to Julian of Norwich (1342–c. 1416) and her revelations of divine love, to Teresa of Ávila (1515–1582) and her ecstatic contemplative union with God, these women all discovered that their longing for transcendence found its fulfillment only in the communion offered through Christ.

Sadly, many women like Ashley have found that even churches have often acquiesced to the dominant spirits of our age. They offer either a disenchanted deism—complete with lessons about niceness from singing CGI vegetables—or force them into an impoverished, counterfeit Christian story that encourages them to shut off all noetic knowing and trade it in for flat, analytical Bible reading as an instructional manual for life. With these as their only options, it is no wonder that many women turn to alternative forms of spirituality that affirm their capacities to pick up on patterns beneath and beyond analytical rationalism.

FROM REENCHANTMENT TO RE-STORYING

Ashley's journey is not an isolated blip on the cultural radar, and it's not just women who share a similar story. We are all longing to move from a state of *closedness* in our souls to a state of *openness.* Over the past five years, I have talked with a number of people whose stories follow a similar trajectory. A new story like Ashley's seems to arise on Substack or YouTube every week these days. Their narrative arcs have followed a similar pattern:

1. SPIRITUAL STARVATION IN A WORLD ABSENT OF WONDER

People long for a mystery they often cannot name. Whether through religious traditions that only offer moral therapeutic deism or through broader cultural narratives that shape our souls toward suspicion and cynicism, we are formed to be *closed* to the Transcendent. Our anti-story incentivizes the *seeing through* with illusory social rewards and acceptance for being the most closed, and thereby the most likely to not be deceived by oppressive authority and power. This masks a deep despair that we arrogantly pass off as profound insight into the true nature of things. "I'm too smart, too enlightened, too woke, too sophisticated to believe that," we're tempted to say.

Our new identity becomes defined by what *we are against* more than what we are *for.* We become increasingly cynical, caught up in an antivision with a heart that hardens so much that it may begin to crack.

2. DESCENT INTO HEDONISM OR NIHILISM

From this place of despair, we either turn toward experiences that can numb the pain and give us pseudo-transcendence or descend into a deepening state of depression. Hedonistic pursuit of pleasure becomes our coping mechanism—a way of simulating the feelings of transcendence. If we're going to live in a show about nothing, then to quote the great Cosmo Kramer from *Seinfeld*, we might as well adopt the motto, "Here's to feeling good all the time." The ancient Greek Epicureans had a similar philosophy. The gods might exist, but they don't really care about us, so the best philosophy in life is to maximize your pleasure.

Others just don't seem to have that party-going constituency, and for better or worse, they use their *seeing through* superpowers to see the emptiness and futility of this kind of escapism. Their disenchanted despair often moves into dark rumination and a spiraling sense of depression. The philosopher Søren Kierkegaard saw both expressions of despair as connected and called them the "despair of not willing to be oneself."[6] For Kierkegaard, the true "authentic self" wasn't a self-authoring agent, but one who realized that the finite must be grounded in the Infinite. The finite human being is made for communion with the Transcendent.

3. MOVEMENT FROM DESPAIR TO DARK REENCHANTMENT

When the heart becomes so hardened that it begins to crack, and when the stories of our secular age no longer seem tenable to live in and the haunting begins to overwhelm, people turn toward transcendent sources of meaning. They move from a state of closedness to a state of openness. There is a hunger for light, for hope, and for a sense of unification to heal their fragmentation. You will rarely find someone who goes off to an ayahuasca retreat and comes back with their cynicism dial turned up to eleven. A number of scientific papers confirm what anecdotal reports have long suggested: Mystical experiences—whether induced by psychedelics or other altered states of consciousness—can lead to measurable increases in openness.[7]

The door reopens to mystery and enchantment, but devoid of a guiding story to function as a map for navigating this newfound spiritual world, many encounter darkness disguised as light. Their openness backfires on them as if a heavily fortified city suddenly tore down all its walls and fired all the watchmen. Perhaps some true light has been allowed in, but so have all sorts of Trojan horses.

This is enchantment, but one that is disordered, unsifted, and untethered from a rubric for discernment.

4. RE-STORYING WITHIN THE TRUE STORY

With the spell of disenchantment broken, people's hearts move from closedness to openness. The taste of transcendence is transformative, even if it is not completely directed toward what truly makes us whole.

The question shifts from not just *if* there is something beyond ourselves but *what* there is. The turn toward transcendence, even at its most chaotic and unfiltered, breaks the hold of the Modern Story and the Postmodern Anti-Story.

Even a turn toward modern expressions of paganism—which spiked from about eight thousand practitioners in America in 1990 to approximately 1.5 million practitioners in 2018—shows signs of a search for a better story to hold our innate longings for transcendence.[8] Catholic philosopher and theologian Bishop Robert Barron, who became a prominent religious voice in the zeitgeist shift through YouTube and podcasting, sees the spike in paganism as a positive sign of a great religious reaching of our souls for some taste of the divine. Joining voices like C. S. Lewis in the twentieth century to Justin Martyr in the second century, Barron argues that the longing for transcendence expressed in paganism isn't wrong, it just needs *fulfillment*.[9]

The danger of dark reenchantment is that it seeks fulfillment and finds sources of meaning and connection that do transcend us, but not everything that transcends us and promises us meaning are *the* Transcendent. What we are seeking is that which *is* of ultimate concern. To paraphrase an argument made by the apostle Paul in his epistle to the Romans, when we settle for any created thing as the source of life deserving of our ultimate concern instead of the Creator—who is the only source of life and is ultimate—our story and world become disordered and dysfunctional. Instead of the wholesome, we experience fragmentation and despair.

To find fulfillment, we need proper orientation. And this orientation requires a map to direct us and show us the pattern and guide us to The Way.

Ashley and countless others have found that as the cultural vibe shifted from closedness to openness, a journey that moved them from despair to meaning, from cynicism to sincerity, and from disenchantment to reenchantment found its deepest fulfillment in The Way of Jesus. This reorientation is a *re-storying* process.

What we are experiencing in the vibe shift is not a singular, momentary epiphany but a slow, aching re-storying. We've been stress-testing our guiding stories, nostalgically going back to sift out what gold remains, and learning to let die that which does not lead to life. Our gods are dying, and with them the lie that we can live without a map. We've seen that there is no storyless life. We are always moving, as stories do, from some beginning to some end, so which end will we be oriented toward? Orientation is inevitable.

We are always being storied by something. And we are always orienting ourselves toward some end. What we're witnessing in the zeitgeist shift is the slow, aching realization that our storyless age has reached its limit. The anti-story has failed to nourish us. The postmodern detour has led not to liberation but to civilizational decline. Game A is collapsing.

As our hearts move from closedness to openness, from disillusionment to desire, we're rediscovering something ancient yet new: The deepest fulfillment of our longing is not just transcendence but belonging in a story that names good and evil, life and death, as well as holds all our desires for meaning, sets the world right, and stands the test of all times.

CHAPTER 12

Religious Renaissance

It kept happening, for months. Christ to the left of me, Christ to the right. It was unnerving. I turned away again and again, but every time I looked back, he was still there. I began to feel I was being . . . hunted?

Paul Kingsnorth

At the age of fifteen, Paul Kingsnorth wandered into a quiet medieval church with some friends. His family had never gone to church growing up; nonetheless, even as a professed teenage atheist, he found something hauntingly beautiful about stepping inside a church. There was *something* here that he couldn't find anywhere else in his home country of England. On this particular day, the young Kingsnorth didn't choose sincere reverence, but the kind of performative, angsty, ironic mockery that would have been in fashion among the hippest of British writers in the '80s. In the visitors' book inside the old church, he scribbled in jagged black ink: "I WILL DESTROY YOU AND ALL YOUR WORKS—SATAN."

In the moment, he chalked it up to simple teenage tomfoolery, but years later, he'd see it differently. The macroculture known as Western civilization has trace elements of the Christian story in its underlying code. Kingsnorth, like so many of us, knew the hymns and Bible stories even though he did not believe in them. As he grew older, his own story began to follow the same narrative arc we saw in Ashley Lande's journey—spiritual starvation and despair moving into reenchantment, closedness moving into openness.

For Kingsnorth, that openness to transcendence led him to environmental activism, to Zen silence and meditation, and to becoming a pagan priest. He practiced Wiccan rituals in moonlit forests and toyed with magic. He was a respected writer, and, unbeknownst to most, many of the great British mythmakers of our generation had a less-than-secretive relationship to dark magic rituals.

Alan Moore, known for *Watchmen* and *V for Vendetta*, openly identifies as a ceremonial magician and claims to have received inspiration for his stories from Roman gods and demons. Grant Morrison, whose revamped *All-Star Superman* stories were one inspiration for James Gunn's 2025 big-screen reboot of *Superman*, recounts in his best-selling book *Supergods* detailed accounts of magic ceremonies and seances intended to invoke spiritual entities for inspiration. Both men embrace a reenchanted worldview that sees storytelling not merely as entertainment but a form of modern sorcery—a way to access the unseen, conjure transcendent meaning, and transform the spirit of the age through symbol and archetype. Kingsnorth, consciously or unconsciously, had become a disciple of this occult tradition.

But beneath it all was a quiet ache. There was something different about the magic Kingsnorth felt in those old churches he profaned with anti-story energy as a youth. Early in the spring of 2020, that pure white magic began to haunt him again. This time, he found it in the autobiography of Irish philosopher John Moriarty. In the book—entitled *Nostos*, a Greek word meaning "homecoming"—Moriarty told a story of this familiar arc of reenchantment. Spiritual starvation descended into nihilism, and a hardened heart eventually cracked, opening him up to the light of reenchantment. Moriarty had a mystical vision while walking in the mountains one day, and from that taste of transcendence, he went searching for a truth that he could surrender to.

THE STORY THAT HOLDS IT ALL TOGETHER

As Kingsnorth read of Moriarty's revelation, it was as if that same inevitable conclusion was descending upon him as well. In Kingsnorth's own words, "There was only one story that could hold what he had seen."[1] Something was happening to him, and frankly, he didn't like it at all. Reflecting on the kind of desacralized, moral, therapeutic deism he had seen in Christianity as a child, and feeling the tug to step into a guiding story with Christ at the center, holding it all together, perplexed him.

> I didn't know back then that the Christian story is the story of our rebellion against God. I didn't know that by taking part in that rebellion I had become part of the story, whether I liked it or not. I didn't know, either, why Christians see pride as the greatest sin. I only knew that I could argue a good case for the injustice of the world made by this "God," and the silliness of miracles, resurrections, and virgin births. I knew I was cleverer than all the people who believed this sort of rubbish, and I was happy to tell them so.[2]

Paul Kingsnorth had been shaped by the anti-story but chalked it up to his own cleverness—a common side effect of the hidden, soul-shaping deception of the anti-story. He had become a "priest of the witch gods," but now a crucified God-Man had started haunting his dreams. He was resisting the pull toward this Christ, like some sci-fi starship caught within the invisible tug of a giant tractor beam. Then one night, as he was out to dinner with his wife, she looked at him and said, with all of the clairvoyant ability the feminine soul has been fine-tuned to possess, "You're going to become a Christian."

It was an odd statement that came out of the conversational blue, but Kingsnorth knew that his wife had a penchant for the noetic and was right more than he liked to admit. A slow conversion of his soul was happening, and the hauntings did not stop there. Kingsnorth describes the unfolding experiences in his essay "The Cross and the Machine":

> It kept happening, for months. Christ to the left of me, Christ to the right. It was unnerving. I turned away again and again, but every time I looked back, he was still there. I began to feel I was being . . . hunted? I wanted it to stop; at least, I thought I did. I had no interest in Christianity. I was a witch! A Zen witch, in fact, which I thought sounded pretty damned edgy. But I knew who was after me, and I knew it wasn't over.[3]

Eventually, the cynical engines that had sought to pull him out of this holy tractor beam broke down. At a children's music recital, of all places, love broke in. In an instant, everything everywhere all at once was connected. The creation he had loved so dearly and sought to redeem in environmental activism and pagan cosplay in enchanted forests was now pulsing with meaning. The right and left hemispheric knowing came together, and he saw one story holding it all together with that crucified God-Man who haunted his dreams at the center of it all.

Kingsnorth was eventually baptized in the icy waters of Shannon, England. His enchanted world had now found its proper orientation. Every longing for transcendence he experienced in nature and in Wicca found its fulfillment in the transcendent God who had taken on matter and nature in the incarnation of Christ. God in this sacred story is both transcendent and immanent, which brought everything together for Kingsnorth, who could neither deny the beauty and goodness of the natural world nor settle for a story in which the material stuff of the world is all we have. In a 2022 conversation with Anglican theologian Rowan Williams and author/podcaster Justin Brierley, Kingsnorth described his conversion as a kind of *returning*. It was not that he had once inhabited this story and then left it behind; rather, he realized that this was the true story which we all come from, and stepping into it felt like a homecoming.[4]

Kingsnorth would eventually begin to worship in an Eastern Orthodox church. Others who are experiencing a homecoming and a return to meaning are worshiping in Catholic cathedrals, with Anglican liturgies, at Charismatic revivals, or in old Baptist churches with tall steeples. Data is slowly beginning to catch up with the anecdotes of the Jordan Halls, Ashley Landes, and Paul Kingsnorths of culture, but the evidence is becoming undeniable.

A Religious Renaissance is beginning.

A SEARCH FOR THE WAY THAT LEADS TO LIFE

The post-cynical wave has brought with it a culture-wide awakening that the way we've been living doesn't lead to life. As if we were the prodigal son of Jesus' famous parable, who found himself eating the slop of pigs after burning through his inheritance, we've awoken in the muck with hungry bellies, realizing that there *was* a better life than this . . . even if we can't fully remember where we came from. Some are being drawn to this homecoming not only through mystical experiences but also through the frightening realization that every mental simulation of Game A we run seems to end in a disastrous "game over." *Mad Max*, *Terminator*, *The Matrix*, *Blade Runner*, *The Hunger Games*, *1984*—every scenario we imagine seems to end in pig slop for dinner.

But even as Paul Kingsnorth observed while visiting the beautiful but mostly empty churches of his youth, the underlying code in our civilization is not completely devoid of the Story of stories. When the anti-story swung its deconstructing sledgehammer throughout our culture, killing Superman in the process, the new gods that rushed to fill the vacuum only seemed to speed up our descent into the pig slop. In that process, many began to realize that the positive values we believed were just universal, like sacrificial care for the least of these, the inherent dignity of the human person, and the unction to forgive those who have done wrong but are penitent, are, in fact, *not* universal to every culture's guiding stories.

These values were baked into our civilizational code through some degree of adherence to the Christian story, and a significant turning point in our zeitgeist shift has come from the realization that discarding the Christian story, in whatever measure we adhered to it, didn't make things better. Deconstructing that story unplugged us from the very foundations of the moral world that held us together. Even after a relatively short sprint of attempting to build post-Christian utopias, we realized that the further we moved away from that story, the worse our society got.

An influential book that inadvertently turned many people away from amorphous spirituality or nihilistic deconstruction and toward the Religious Renaissance is written by historian (but not Spider-Man) Tom Holland. In his 2019 *Dominion: How the Christian Revolution Remade the World*, Holland traced the arc of Western civilization from the ancient Greeks and Romans to the modern day and made an uncomfortable discovery as a self-described agnostic. The moral framework he cherished in our care for the vulnerable, our foundational affirmation of the sacred worth of the individual, and the call to the powerful to serve didn't come from Athens or Rome. It came from Golgotha.

The ideas that the first shall be last and the last shall be first, that the victim of injustice has moral authority over the oppressive victor, and that the Homelanders of the world who exalt themselves will be laid low are ideas the ancient Romans would have mocked. It's part of the reason why they loathed the strange philosophy of the ancient Christians in their empire.

The greatest of all Greek philosophers, Plato, on at least two occasions described the Greek practice of discarding babies that were unsightly, deformed, and didn't seem worth caring for. Plato wasn't upset by this. In fact, he argued for infanticide to be part of the perfect utopian state. His most famous student, Aristotle, agreed. Holland argues that if we find this behavior morally repugnant, it is because the Christian story has become so embedded in our cultural stories, institutions, laws, and modern protest movements that our moral imaginations are shaped to find it repugnant.

Ancient Rome, one of the greatest empires that ever existed, didn't even build hospitals for its citizens. The first true hospital was built by Christians in the fourth century and was called the Basileias after Basil of Caesarea, who saw in the Christian story a central calling to care for the sick and the poor. The Roman sexual ethic taught men of power to see women, slaves, and even children as mere objects of sexual gratification. You could pass around every possible rumor of Harvey Weinstein or Jeffrey Epstein to the most respectable of ancient Romans, and nearly all of them would go, "So what's the big deal?" Mutual consent, marital fidelity, and sexual restraint are not universal norms. They are implications of the Christian story, and they transformed Western civilization.

When the New Atheists like Richard Dawkins argued that we could do away with Christianity and be ushered into a utopian future, they found out the hard way that these supposedly secular ethics baked into our culture are not the default disposition of human nature. Tom Holland reminded our culture that these values are Christian. These days, Dawkins seems far more concerned with cancel culture and the post-truth world undercutting his love for science than he does with railing against Christianity like he did circa 2005. On Easter Sunday of 2024, Dawkins even admitted his preference for a civilization that has the Christian story baked into its cultural code when he publicly confessed, "I like to live in a culturally Christian country, even if I don't believe a single word of Christian faith."[5]

When Canadian psychologist and cultural provocateur Jordan Peterson continued to follow the thread of his lectures on biblical stories, evolutionary psychology, and the archetypal patterns buried in the greatest stories of all time, he increasingly saw a pattern emerging—a gravitational center pulling the narrative arc of civilization into alignment. Beneath myths, literature, dreams, and even modern heroes' journeys, there seemed to be one story quietly scaffolding them all, one symbol standing as the hinge of the whole tradition: the Cross of Christ.

Peterson, initially cautious and almost reluctant, began to suggest—first between the lines, then more directly—that the crucifixion of Christ was not just a religious claim but the central mythos of our civilizational consciousness. Echoing the confessions of both Kingsnorth and Holland, Peterson began to argue directly that the Cross of Christ was the axis around which all our myths and cultural narratives might intersect with history to announce, "This is what reality is."

In a 2021 conversation between Peterson and the influential Eastern Orthodox public intellectual Jonathan Pageau, Peterson confessed that he was "terrified" as to what all of his lifelong research to find a map of meaning was pointing to:

> But the difference, and C. S. Lewis pointed this out as well, the difference between those mythological gods and Christ was that there's a historical representation of his existence as well . . .
>
> So what you have in the figure of Christ is an actual person who actually lived, plus a myth, and in some sense, Christ is the union of those two things. The problem is that I probably believe that. But I don't know . . . I'm amazed at my own belief, and I don't understand it.
>
> Because . . . I've seen . . . sometimes, the objective world and the narrative world touch. You know that's Jungian synchronicity. And I've seen that many times in my own life. And so in some sense, I believe it's undeniable, you know, we have a narrative sense of the world. For me, that's been the world of morality. That's the world that tells us how to act. It's real. Like, we treat it like it's real. It's not the objective world. But the narrative and the objective world touch. And the ultimate example of that in principle is supposed to be Christ. But I don't know what to . . . that seems to me oddly plausible. But I still don't know what to make of it. It's too [breaking down in tears] . . . partly because it's too terrifying a reality to fully believe. I don't even know what would happen to you if you fully believed it.[6]

In Holland's analysis of history and Peterson's psychoanalysis of Western stories, there was an apocalyptic problem our culture had to face. Without a cruciform center, the post-Christian world would not become more humane; it would become more pagan. Not in a New Age–adjacent, dress-up-in-the-woods-and-chant-in-a-drum-circle sense, but in the Nietzschean-like sense of that ancient Roman world where the will to power fills the vacuum, leaving the strong to do what they will while the weak suffer what they must.

A strange chorus began to rise in our allegedly post-Christian culture: Historians, psychologists, public intellectuals, mystics, and misfits were simultaneously suggesting that the best compass we have to point us toward true north might be the Christian story. While the symbolic scaffolding of society was breaking, even those who did not go to church themselves were publicly asking aloud: "What if going back to church might actually save us?"

While some, like popular YouTube atheist Alex O'Connor, suggested this spike in interest in Christianity was really just political conservatives using elements of Christianity for their agenda (which obviously does happen), others like Justin Brierley, author and host of *The Surprising Rebirth of God* book and podcast, have demonstrated numerous examples of why O'Connor isn't seeing the full picture of what is really going on with our Religious Renaissance.

Brierley has cited numerous cases that show this vibe shift can't be reduced to our impoverished culture war heuristic of red team versus blue team. Take reports that began coming from the campus of the University of Oxford in 2025 as one example. A quiet religious revival was beginning to stir that had some nones taking to Reddit to voice their shock at how, as one Redditor put it, "People who were very atheist and left wing . . . have become super religious since attending the University."[7]

Voices from both the political left and right, whether they were concerned with environmental collapse or a sexual revolution that threatened to return us to pagan sexual ethics, were tracking through different paths to the same haunting realization: If we abandon the story that made us, we may all find ourselves eating in a dystopian pig trough.

A CULTURAL HOMECOMING

Even if our culture doesn't know what to make of all the metaphysical claims of orthodox Christian theology, there is strong evidence that a longing for homecoming and re-storying within the Christian story is happening. Sociologist Ryan Burge noted in 2024 that after three decades of consistent increases in the number of nones in America, there has been a surprising plateau. This has coincided with a significant spike in church attendance among Gen Z men, with numbers surpassing women—something that has never happened in the recorded religious history of America.[8] The trend of male Zoomers returning to church isn't just an American phenomenon either. It's happening throughout the West.

In Australia, 39 percent of male Zoomers now self-identify as Christian—a number 11 percent higher than their female counterparts.[9] In the UK, reports of significant spikes in church attendance among Gen Z hit news headlines as well. While the UK data is still being sorted and evaluated, many of the firsthand accounts from local pastors point to a similar trend seen in the land down under: Young men appear to be leading the way.[10] The crisis of meaning, whether felt at the individual level or on a civilizational scale, is driving a reversal of three decades of religious decline, and it feels, in some ways, as if this shift has happened overnight. There's something going on with Gen Z, and especially Gen Z men, but it isn't just with them.

Glen Scrivener, Anglican minister and host of the podcast *Speak Life*, has been tracking this sudden Religious Renaissance and tells the story of a Millennial man who turned up at his church "out of the blue" one Sunday morning. They started talking about what had brought him to church, and the man confessed he realized the Christian story had played some foundational role in all that was good about Western culture. If all he saw as true, good, and beautiful in his culture had its origins in the Christian story, then he figured he'd better purchase a Bible and visit his local church.

Scrivener assumed the man had reached this conclusion by reading Tom Holland's *Dominion*, and asked him, "So how long have you been on the Tom Holland train?" Perplexed, the man responded, "What's Spider-Man got to do with it?" He had never read the book or heard Holland's thesis.[11] This was an epiphany that felt as if it were just in the air—a realization of pattern beneath the stories and values of his culture. The man was picking up on a vibe. This was a zeitgeist shift.

Bible sales in the US are up 40 percent since 2019, with a 22 percent increase between 2022 and 2024 alone.[12] Weekly church attendance among Gen Xers and Millennials in America has risen to levels well beyond prepandemic levels, especially among Millennials, who have seen a nearly 20 percent jump since 2019.[13] The churches they are returning to aren't pushing them to keep deconstructing tradition or swap out the wisdom of the past for postmodern cynicism. The stories flooding our social networks, and the new data catching up to corroborate these testimonies, point to something different.

Peruse countless videos from an unlikely underground YouTube star named Paul Vander Klay, and you'll notice a pattern. Vander Klay is a white-bearded Boomer pastor in a dying California church who took to YouTube in 2017 to talk about the shifting dialogue around religion that he was noticing online. He started hosting local meetups with nones and collecting the stories of people of all ages who shared a similar story arc of moving from closedness to openness to the Christian story. You'd be hard-pressed to find in any of the numerous personal stories he collected a single case where these spiritual sojourners found meaning in a church stuck in the postmodern mode of suspicion.

What they are returning to are churches with a deep sense of tradition, wonder, and enchantment that doesn't fit neatly within the Modern Story or the Postmodern Anti-Story. They aren't looking for moral therapeutic deism nestled inside a rock-and-roll concert with a side of Christian karaoke. They're looking for what John Mark McMillan, Jordan Hall, "Thomas," Ashley Lande, and Paul Kingsnorth found. Even though each of these people worships in a different denominational context, a common current flows beneath it all. They want to be anchored in a story that has stood the test of time, not in a novelty that tries to reinvent itself every week. And there's data to support these anecdotes too.

Orthodox churches reported that in 2022 and 2023, the rate of new converts doubled compared with the annual average from 2013 to 2019.[14] The Anglican Church in North America reported a 12 percent increase in attendance in 2023, surpassing prepandemic levels.[15] Even nondenominational Charismatic churches are reexploring more ancient and liturgical practices of worship in this vibe shift.

The thriving Everyday Church, a Charismatic church in Minneapolis that has experienced explosive growth for years, primarily among Millennials and Gen Zers, consecrated the opening of its new sanctuary and prayer room in 2024 with a processional led by the elements of the Eucharist. This ushered in a weekly practice of Communion, a ritual often associated with more "high church" traditions like Catholic Mass, and was mingled with the typical Charismatic and Pentecostal practices of ecstatic singing, praying for the sick, and discerning the Spirit's voice. As I've talked with national leaders in the Vineyard Movement, an association of Charismatic-evangelical churches, they report similar shifts toward integrating more ancient Christian practices and theology across their family of churches.[16]

INCARNATION AND THE SPIRIT OF THE AGE

People aren't running away from the traditions they were culturally programmed to deconstruct; they're running toward them. Efforts to make the Christian story neatly fit the Modern Story or the Postmodern Anti-Story failed, and if you're stuck filtering the world through one of those two lenses, none of this will make sense. Is this a full-on return to the Traditional Story? No, it's not that either.

To understand what is happening, you need to understand how the true Pattern always functions *incarnationally*—that is to say, the Story always works *within* culture. It doesn't create its own culture, and the real thing doesn't conquer cultures with Nietzschean will to power. This Story reorients cultures toward the true fulfillment of their deepest longings.

This is why the epicenter of the Christian story has never been bound to one location or culture. From the Middle East and North Africa to Rome, from Byzantium to Western Europe, from North America to the African continent and throughout Asia, no single people, empire, or culture has laid exclusive claim to this Story. It has transcended all and transformed all.

What Christ is doing now in an increasingly metamodern culture will look different from what happened in the modern and postmodern eras. The Story will retain its eternally true pattern, but how it incarnates this cultural moment will be different.

All of what we've been seeing and sensing is connected. The sincerity you didn't fully realize you missed until *Everything Everywhere All at Once* named the ache for something beyond irony and nihilism in 2022. The thing that made you go, "That's what movies used to feel like" after you walked out of *Top Gun: Maverick* in that same year. The feeling you got when you stopped caring if Creed was cool and allowed yourself to post-ironically belt out, "Can you take me higher?" The haunting suspicion you get while staring at your children that maybe love isn't just an evolutionary illusion. The sudden realization while sitting in a personal or civilizational pig trough that a homecoming should be our next chapter.

Metamodernism, reenchantment, the Religious Renaissance—all of it is connected. A culture-wide reorientation is underway. Spiritual closedness, with all its cynicism, detachment, and disenchantment, is giving way to spiritual openness with all its fresh hope, sincerity, wholesomeness, belonging, and Communion.

This is a zeitgeist shift—a "spirit of the age" shift—in the deepest sense of the term. The Spirit beckons us to live in the Story that discloses the very structure of reality itself, echoed in our most profound myths and stories, and even in the cycles of the world we once dubbed as "natural" but now feel are teeming with magic.

Does it matter if you don't know what to make of the metaphysics and doctrines, as long as you're living *as if* it were true? Maybe our vibe shift is helping us see something true about the Story that we couldn't see in modern and postmodern culture.

Could it even transform your days that so often feel like a show about nothing into a show filled with the sacred and meaningful?

CHAPTER 13

Based on a True Story

Belief is when your whole being is set
to act as if something is so.
Dallas Willard

We've seen that a vibe shift has been moving across our culture, releasing us from our cynical prisons, opening us up to the wholesome, and cracking open a spiritual canopy that had been closed for far too long. Cynicism imploded under the weight of its own emptiness. Sincerity snuck back into the party wearing a post-ironic Creed shirt.

Even the idea of the "spiritual," which had been banished to the margins of society where only the Appalachian snake handlers and the people who shop at Whole Foods hang out, began to haunt us again. The meaning crisis and civilizational decline exposed the need for a better guiding story, and many started finding it in the God we'd previously thought was dead.

A quiet revival is underway, and it's getting louder. It's even got Richard Dawkins proclaiming that the Christian story makes the world better. Take a DeLorean back to 2008 to tell me this would happen in the future, and I would tell you that you're crazy, McFly.

But is re-storying within the Christian story the right move? That's not a question any of us can afford to table any longer.

We are storied creatures. That's not poetic fluff—it's a scientific and existential reality. You don't live by cold facts and data. You live by narrative, and some story is already shaping you. Best-selling books like James Clear's *Atomic Habits* and John Mark Comer's *Practicing the Way* are making this point abundantly clear to the masses: The story you live into with your day-to-day decisions is the story you become.

So, what story would you rather become?

Maybe you start with the question of, "Well, what story works?" But you don't just want what *works* in the sense of what makes you rich or pretty. That nihilistic abyss swallows up rich people too. Pretty won't get you far if this all goes *The Last of Us* out there.

No, what you're really looking for in a guiding story that works is a story that is big enough to carry the weight of your existence and the salvation of the world. That's a much heavier question, but the longer you push off answering it, the worse the despair becomes and the more likely it is that we inch a little bit closer to live-reenacting *Thunderdome* on a civilizational scale.

If what the psychologists have said so far is true—that human beings are storied creatures and that meaning requires coherence, purpose, and significance—then figuring out what story we should live in is not a secondary matter. It's the most important decision we could ever make.

So, I'll ask once again: Is the Christian story coherent?

THE PATTERN IS EVERYWHERE

Sure, Christianity as an organized religion has only been around for a couple thousand years, but the unique claim of the great Christian visionaries has been that the Story is older than language itself. As G. K. Chesterton argued, it is the Story that every Stone Age cave painting ached for. Early Christians like Justin Martyr said the seeds of this Story could be found in every true insight of the Greek philosophers.

But how can this be? Cavemen didn't paint pictures of crosses, and Plato wasn't rocking WWJD bracelets four hundred years before Jesus' virgin birth. It helps to have a metamodern way of seeing so we're not just looking for a pattern, but seeing across patterns for a Pattern of patterns, a Story of stories.

If you look through this metamodern lens, you begin to notice that the Story surfaces not just in scriptures and stained-glass windows, but in black holes and burned forests, in ancient mythic epics and modern Marvel scripts. It is the pattern of death and resurrection. Of descent and return. Of losing your life only to find it, and the hope that history will eventually end with a happily ever after. The Pattern keeps showing up everywhere, not because it's a clever literary device, but because it's embedded in the center of reality itself.

It is a grand claim—perhaps the grandest of all. It is the claim that the crucified God-Man who haunted Paul Kingsnorth's dreams is the reference note that tunes the music of the spheres. It is the Story that divides the light and shadow and affirms when we have experienced a resonance with the wholesome. It was in the code of Western civilization, producing all that's good about our culture, but it is not reducible to being just the story of the West.

Like all epic myths of all civilizations, both great and small, this Story is the fulfillment of each of their longings. Osiris. Dionysus. Persephone. Even Superman. It's death and resurrection—a phoenix that bursts into flame and is reborn from the ashes. Behind Tony Stark's "I am Iron Man" snap that saves the world in his sacrifice, Cooper's loving descent into an interstellar abyss, and Harry Potter's death and return from the grave is the true Pattern we cannot escape, no matter how long we've tried to run from it.

What Jung called the archetype, what Campbell saw in the Hero's Journey as the hero descended into the abyss and rose back up in resurrection power, what Tolkien called the eucatastrophe, where, in all the great stories, a seemingly inevitable tragedy is interrupted by a sudden, joyful reversal—this is what Christians dare to call *history*.

The myth becomes fact. The archetype becomes flesh. And the patterns of nature and myth find their fulfillment in the Story.

Open a seed pod and watch it fall to the ground and die. Then, and only then, will it be able to bear fruit. Compost becomes the cradle of new life. Forest fires clear the way for wildflowers. Stars collapse into black holes or explode into supernovae, scattering the heavy elements that make planets and people possible.

It's *kenosis* all the way down.

KENOSIS AT THE CENTER

Kenosis is a Greek term that ancient Christians believed captured what was at the center of the Story; it is the pattern of self-giving love, the voluntary emptying of power and prestige for the good of another that we see in the incarnation, death, and resurrection of Christ. It is a God who descends in kenotic love.

Kenotic love is the movement of sacrificial descent that intends to raise up another with it. This sacrificial descent is not a movement of self-destruction. It is the willing emptying that creates space for union. This Story, with kenosis at its center, was among the earliest songs written by Christians in the first century and was recorded in Philippians 2:6–11. And this Story, which we see in that ancient Christ hymn, can be seen everywhere.

Particles interact by sharing, organisms cooperate by limiting themselves for the sake of the whole, and human life is conceived through self-emptying and opening, both giving a seed and receiving it. This new life grows in a mother's womb through kenotic love as she sacrificially shares the very food she brings into her body to raise up the new life within her. Each new threshold of complexity in the cosmos—matter, life, consciousness—emerges through the giving away of some measure of independence in exchange for deeper belonging, of interdependence.

Relationship. Loving, mutual self-emptying. Union and Communion. Kenosis is at the heart of reality.

Even people who claim that they don't believe in the Christian story talk like this. They say things like, "I felt like I had to die to who I was before I could really live." Or, "I had to let go of the version of myself I was clinging to." Even at the center of all that works in therapy culture is the pattern of death and resurrection. There is always some form of descent, surrender, and loss before renewal, reintegration, and life.

Why does this work? Because that kenotic love is at the core of reality. The Story is not only coherent—it is the pattern that both myth and nature adhere to.

The writers of the New Testament understood that while Christ absolutely was a flesh-and-blood first-century rabbi who worked miracles, was crucified under Pontius Pilate, died, and rose again, he was the incarnation of that which had always existed even before the first Christmas: "In the beginning was the Word, and the Word was with God, and the Word was God. He was with God in the beginning. Through him all things were made; without him nothing was made that has been made. In him was life, and that life was the light of all mankind. The light shines in the darkness, and the darkness has not overcome it."[1]

John begins his gospel with a cosmic creation story and uses the Greek term *logos*, translated here as "Word," to refer to Christ. *Logos* was already pregnant with meaning for John's audience. In that ancient world, the Logos was understood to be the logic of the cosmos, the ordering principle that makes reality coherent and knowable.[2] Our very ability to discern patterns as a pattern-hunting species is because we hunt for the Logos. The claim of the Christian story is that Pattern which grounds all patterns and makes anything knowable at all is Christ—the Logos made flesh.

And this wasn't just a "start it and let it run on its own" act of creation either. That's deism. Other New Testament writers describe Christ as "holding all things together" and "sustaining all things." For seventh-century theologian Maximus the Confessor, everything in creation reflects a little piece of the Logos—what he called the *logoi*—and these pieces of the Pattern, which reside in each of us, were designed to be drawn back to their source. Every glimpse of truth, goodness, or beauty that you're getting in this present moment comes from one source holding it all together.

So not only is the Story coherent—it's where any sense of coherence comes from.

But to be clear, making sense of all these metaphysical claims isn't a prerequisite for stepping into the Story. What if your journey is like Jordan Hall, who just followed a wholesome vibe to a little country church even while his prefrontal cortex was telling him, "Dude. You don't actually believe this stuff . . ."?

Or what if you're like the guy who showed up at Glen Scrivener's church and pretty much told him, "All I know is that things seem to be better when people live *as if* they were Christian"? Once again, this is where our metamodern shift might help us.

FAITH IS STEPPING INTO THE STORY

We've been programmed to think about religion as this odd separate filing cabinet detached from real life. In this cabinet, you sort through all your propositional beliefs about God, the Bible, virgin births, and strange end-times theories that include a lot of charts. Check the correct boxes on the forms and submit them to some DMV clerk in the heavens, and you're now on the right team and can start doing the right stuff.

But this way of viewing faith would have been completely foreign to nearly anyone living before the Modern Story. Thankfully, the vibe shift is also changing the way we think about what it means to live in the Story and helping us to recover this ancient, holistic perspective. It's not just about believing facts about a story, like agreeing with data points you enter into a spreadsheet, nor is it only about *seeing through* false stories.

Stepping into the Story has always been the central feature of faith.

We just lost sight of it somewhere along the way. And we find out the Story is true only by *acting as if* it were true and stepping into it.

This is why books like John Mark Comer's *Practicing the Way* are flying off the shelves and why churches that have a high value for time-tested rituals are attracting those who are hungry for reconstruction. They understand that rituals and practices change our stories from the bottom up. To paraphrase Carl Jung, and I think the apostle Paul would agree, it's not that people have stories as much as stories have people.

This is why early Christians called their new way of life together "the Way." It wasn't a cold calculation, and it wasn't a written test that you passed or failed—it was a path to walk. It was a way of seeing the world, of living in your flesh-and-blood body, of treating other people, of structuring time, of orienting your heart. You could only know it by living it.

In the Gospel of Matthew, there's a fascinating story that illustrates this. In this scene, Jesus's disciples are out fishing at night on the Sea of Galilee as the wind grows stronger and the waves begin to toss the boat around. Not long before dawn, an apparition to their senses, which has been clouded by the storm and darkness, appears on the lake. The terrified disciples scream out like it's an episode of *Scooby-Doo*, "It's a ghost!"

But the voice upon the lake says back, "Take courage! It is I. Don't be afraid."[3] It is the voice of Christ who has been walking on the waves, but they didn't realize that. Peter, one of Jesus' most headstrong disciples, thinks it may be the voice of his master and says, "Lord, if it's you, tell me to come to you on the water." The haunting apparition's only response? "Come."[4]

So Peter steps out, takes his first few steps upon the sea, panics, falls into the water, and is rescued by Christ, who meets him on the waves. Peter discovers that this is Christ not by conducting a scientific experiment in a lab on whether God-Men can walk on water, nor does he discover it by perpetually doubting within the safe confines of the boat. Instead he discovers the living Logos only by stepping out of the boat. Peter acted *as if* it were true.

C. S. Lewis, one of the most prescient intellectual voices of the twentieth century, experienced his own re-storying. In many ways, Lewis's own journey followed the familiar arc we've begun to see more frequently in today's Religious Renaissance. Spiritual starvation pulled him out of disenchanted Christianity in his youth, moving him into despair and closedness in atheistic materialism, only to eventually be reenchanted within a more holistic Christian story that satisfied both his longing for meaning and his intellectual curiosity.

While Lewis put together a number of compelling left-brained propositional arguments for his modernist readers, inviting them to trust that the Story was true (most notably in *Mere Christianity*), he ultimately knew that it was only by stepping into the Story that we *truly* come to know. In his essay "Meditation in a Toolshed," Lewis tells an illuminating parable. He describes standing in a dark toolshed where a singular beam of sunlight shines through a crack at the top of the doorframe. "I was seeing the beam, not seeing things by it. Then I moved, so that the beam fell on my eyes. Instantly, the whole previous picture vanished." By *stepping into* the light, Lewis experienced a profound transformation of perspective. The utter darkness that once surrounded him gave way to sheer illumination. By looking "along the beam," he saw, beyond the shed, the living trees swaying in the wind. Beyond that, this beam of light traveled millions of miles from the radiant epicenter of our solar system—the sun.

For Lewis, this experience of "looking along the beam" was different from merely looking at it from the outside, so that any truly reasonable person must confront the question of, "Which is the 'true' or 'valid' experience? Which tells you most about the thing?"[5]

Looking at the light from the outside is very different from stepping into it and looking from within. The *stepping into* gives us a different kind of knowing because it changes our relationship to the light. What Christians have long called "faith" has always been about stepping into the light, not signing off on a list of propositions we agree with.

Listening to a love song or watching a romantic movie might give you some sense of knowing what love is, but it isn't the same knowing as that first taste of falling in love with a real person. It isn't the same knowledge of love as being married for decades and living through the ups and downs, the joys and disappointments. We can never have that kind of *knowing* by just looking at the beam. There are some things you can only understand from inside.

As philosopher Esther Meek argues, to know anything at all is to enter into a kind of loving relationship with it, but in our age of endless options, we can get existentially stuck in a mode of perpetually swiping right and never making a decision to commit. This is a perennial human problem, but it is exacerbated in our digital age.[6]

Yet indecision is itself a decision. The disciples who stayed in the boat made a choice. Whether out of fear, comfort, or calculated caution, they chose to withhold trust and remain spectators to something they couldn't yet explain. And in doing so, they cut themselves off from the kind of knowing that only comes from getting out of the boat.

Waiting for some form of absolute certainty before intentionally stepping into a story is especially dangerous in our age of hyperconnectivity. The flood of options we have to choose from can be paralyzing. Americans spend, on average, five hours a day staring at their smartphones. The average US household watches more than forty-three hours of video a week across all devices.[7] We may not feel like we are actively and intentionally choosing a story to live in through these daily habits, but remember—people don't have stories so much as stories have people. We are being shaped by some story, whether we're consciously aware of it or not.

HOW STORIES ARE FORMED IN US

We don't get to choose whether or not we'll be shaped by a guiding story; we just get to choose which one. Cognitive science has shown that our brains are constantly building internal models of the world, not just through abstract thought, but through what we attend to, repeat, and embody. Every time you open your phone, scroll a feed, binge a show, or follow a media cycle, you are practicing a liturgy. That liturgy is rehearsing a story about what matters, what a good life looks like, who the heroes and villains are, and what kind of person you should be. Some story is having you. And we can inhabit a story in one of two ways: through *passive story formation* or *active story formation*.

Passive story formation happens to you by sheer proximity to what you scroll past, laugh at, mimic, or emotionally absorb without thinking. Remember the concept of mean world syndrome from back in chapter 2? Mean world syndrome is a cognitive bias where people who frequently consume dark and violent media tend to overestimate how violent the world actually is. For example, did you know that murder rates in the US today are not worse than they were thirty years ago? In fact, they are substantially better and are comparable to what they were back in the early 1950s.

Now, what makes most of us think that murder rates are now worse than they were back in the *Leave It to Beaver* days? Unless you've actively done crime statistics research, you may have concluded that there are far more murders per capita today. That's just how passive story formation works in us. We have access to a 24/7 cable news cycle, can spend hours doomscrolling each day, and have an ever-expanding catalog of violent shows and movies to thank for distorting our picture of reality.

Non-formation is never an option, especially in our information age. Even the word "information" comes from the Latin *informare*, which means "to give shape or form."[8] This should remind us that information is always formative. It's just a matter of to what end.

If we don't want our information age to shape us into a story that leads to more meaning crisis and a *Terminator*-style dystopian future, especially when Silicon Valley and China are in an AI arms race to pretty much build Skynet, then we'd better step into the right story through the process of active story formation, or the choice to be intentionally formed by a story that is worthy of your ultimate concern.

It means putting yourself in environments, habits, and relationships that conform to the Story. At the heart of active story formation is the decision to *act as if.*

ACT AS IF YOU'RE IN LOVE

Act as if and you might find, like Jordan Hall did, that your story starts changing for the better. Go to a boring little church that at least slightly haunts you and slightly embarrasses you. Sing loudly, even if you don't know what to make of all the words. Bring a casserole to the potluck. Pray the Lord's Prayer when you start your day. Some days you might feel magic, and other days you won't. But if you never commit, you'll never know whether the Story really works.

It's been pretty dark inside our little cultural toolshed for decades. Maybe that's why we find ourselves especially drawn to the light—to the wholesome and the sincere. That Creed concert isn't salvation . . . I mean, it might be close, but the urge to let go of cynicism and maybe even allow yourself to say something sincere is like the light beckoning you to step inside.

Maybe that's why an episode of *Joe Pera Talks with You*, like the one where Joe quietly explains the joy of taking a fall drive in the Midwest to take in all the colors of the changing trees, can feel like an unexpected altar call to the post-cynical soul. Although it doesn't use any explicit religious language, the invitation to gratefulness, awe, and wonder at the mundane beauty that surrounds us, even in the colorful death and resurrection of local maple trees, creates an opportunity for a profoundly religious experience. Something in us is picking up on the Pattern. The seeds of the Logos are here too.

In the Christian tradition, many would say that we experience this resonance as an invitation to *step into* the Story because we are made in the image of God. We are creatures designed for beauty, belonging, and love. The *Imago Dei* doesn't just mean we have rational capacities or moral instincts. It means we're wired to recognize and be drawn toward the light.

The great nineteenth-century philosopher Søren Kierkegaard also understood that the deepest truths don't live in the detached or the abstract. "The crucial thing is to find a truth which is true for me," he wrote.[9] Not because truth is whatever you want it to be, but because truth is only transformative when it's inhabited. Until then, it remains just a possibility. And possibilities can be endlessly deferred.

The deep despair of our cultural meaning crisis can't be defeated by just learning cold, detached facts about Christ, like one might learn facts about Napoleon in history class. It can only be defeated by changing the state of how we relate to the Infinite. *Acting as if* changes the way we relate, and it is this relational change that is at the core of Christian transformation. Peter's stepping out of the boat was more than a cold calculation; it was an act of relational trust.

Am I arguing that we shut down our faculties of reason and just take an irrational leap of faith? No. Again, we have long misunderstood what it even means to be rational. For ancient and medieval Christians, reason could never be divorced from our loves.

Philosopher David Bentley Hart brilliantly captures the relationship between the mind and heart in *All Things Are Full of Gods*. In it, Hart casts the Greek gods Psyche (mind and soul), Eros (love and desire), Hermes (language and meaning), and Hephaistos (materialism) in a hypothetical dialogue about today's pressing philosophical questions regarding mind, consciousness, and God.

Throughout the book, Psyche and Eros are always in agreement. Why? Because the ancients understood better than our Modern Story and Postmodern Anti-Story that mind (Psyche) and heart (Eros) were never meant to be separate. True knowing requires love, because true love orders our reason in the right direction—toward that which is of ultimate concern: God.

Rationality isn't a neutral targeting system. To reason well is to desire well. *How* we relate to something changes the way we see it.

When Peter steps out of the boat, he's not shutting down reason. He's reordering it. He's trusting the deeper coherence of love and the Logos to be in alignment. His reason is being governed by rightly ordered desire, not paralyzed by uncertainty. He is stepping into the true Pattern at the core of reality. He's stepping into the Story.

This is exactly why *acting as if* changes everything. It doesn't bypass reason—it retrains it. It invites the heart and mind into sync, because we come to see clearly only when we love rightly.

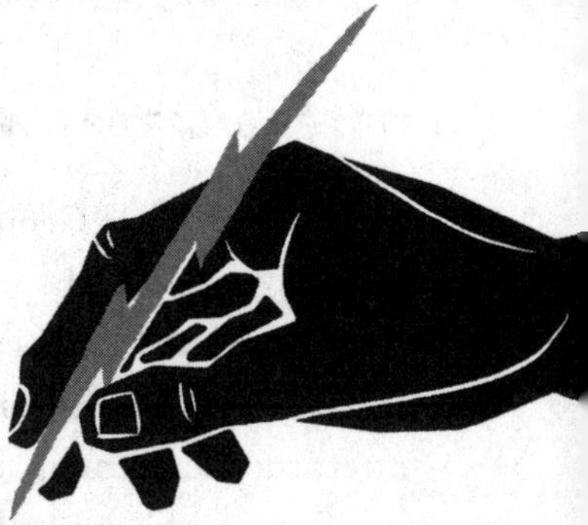

CHAPTER 14

Did You Ever Notice?

Attention, taken to its highest degree,
is the same thing as prayer.
Simone Weil

"Everybody's doing something. We'll do nothing!" was George's famous pitch to Jerry for a "show about nothing" within NBC's monikered show about nothing. Jerry Seinfeld's comedy worked so well in the postmodern pop culture of the '90s because it was predicated on noticing the things that made up the majority of people's lives and pointing out how absurd they were. Comments like "What's the deal with . . ." and "Did you ever notice . . ." were followed by some ridiculous minutiae that made up most of our daily modern lives. While we once believed that we were participating in some coherent, meaningful story of cosmic significance, *Seinfeld* came along at just the right time in the zeitgeist and asked, "Did you ever notice how meaningless it all is?"

But the ironic thing about it was that, especially in the final seasons of the show, these seemingly meaningless moments always connected together for one climactic joke at the end of the episode. In one episode, Kramer picks up a new hobby of trying to hit golf balls on the beach into the Atlantic Ocean, while George works to keep up a lie that Jerry told a college crush about George being a marine biologist. While walking with his date on the beach, people begin to yell that there's a whale stranded near the shore that appears to be dying. A man in the crowd shouts, "Is anyone here a marine biologist?" George's date, believing that George meets those credentials, forces him to help.

Sitting in their regular diner spot together at the end of the episode, George colorfully recalls to Jerry, Elaine, and Kramer how he successfully rescued the whale. "The sea was angry that day, my friends!" he said, describing how he extracted a lone golf ball from the whale's obstructed blowhole. All of the seemingly meaningless and absurd culminated in one absurd punch line.

The brilliance of *Seinfeld* was to call the audience's attention to how much of their own lives were filled with absurdly mundane and seemingly meaningless moments. So many of these moments we inattentively cruise right through on autopilot. When you step back to take note of them and start adding them all up, you begin to realize how much of your life is filled not with heroic action flick scenes, steamy romance, or accomplish-your-dream inspirational montages, but just ordinary *Seinfeld* moments.

Is there really no purpose to most of life, other than some nihilistic punch line? If our lives are filled with so many insignificant moments, then doesn't that make our own stories insignificant? These questions are at the heart of our meaning crisis, and if we're going to rebuild our lives in a better guiding story, that story will have to give those *Seinfeld* moments some sense of purpose and significance. We need to live in a show about *something*.

We've seen the growing hunger in our culture to find a story that can hold our longing for meaning, and how the exhaustion with cynicism and nihilism is giving way to a new cultural longing for sincerity and hope. We know there is a Religious Renaissance happening as people become increasingly aware that we don't have an off switch for our religious impulses. But how does stepping into the Story make our show about something meaningful?

How does stepping into the Christian story affect all these *Seinfeld* moments that fill our lives? Do we suddenly find ourselves out slaying dragons and saving the world every day instead of packing sandwiches for lunch at work, waiting in lines at the DMV, and filing taxes? Not usually, though there certainly are some heroic adventures to be had (which we will explore more of in the final chapter).

Stepping into the Story changes "Did you ever notice how meaningless it all is?" to "Did you ever notice how sacred it all is?" The moments themselves may not change much from an average *Seinfeld* day—you still wait in line for soup, deal with a neighbor's yelping dog waking you in the middle of the night, and maybe even go on a date with someone who never laughs at your jokes—but the way we attend to and interpret those moments change.

ATTENDING RIGHTLY TO THE WORLD

Alexander Schmemann's *For the Life of the World* highlights two potential misunderstandings of what Christian spirituality is all about. Some individuals, still stuck in the Modern Story's separation of secular and religious life, see the religious life as only a *spiritualized inward turn* that uses personal piety and spiritual experiences as a way to escape the mundane *Seinfeld* world. According to Schmemann, this is one of the most common misunderstandings of what stepping into the Christian story looks like.

This kind of spiritual escapism was a major problem for me in my young adult years. Having grown up in a Charismatic and Pentecostal Christian tradition, I never really had problems with believing in magic like others who lived in the kind of moral therapeutic deism Christian subculture that Ashley Lande experienced in her childhood. As I transitioned from my college years into my twenties, I began traveling around the country, helping to lead events and conferences designed to facilitate profound spiritual experiences.

What I wasn't fully aware of was that I had unwittingly ingested a subtle form of gnosticism into my guiding story. The ancient Gnostics were a rival story to the true Story in the first few centuries of Christian history. They believed the material world was the product of a flawed demiurge and that the suffering and emptiness of their lives was a sign that they were called to escape the world. In their rival story, Jesus was never a flesh-and-blood human, but a purely spiritual entity who came to offer secret spiritual knowledge and experiences that would allow people to eventually escape this fundamentally evil world.

Now, I didn't believe those exact gnostic tenets directly, but I had come to believe that the world was more fallen than it was good, that regular life was, like *The Matrix,* a prison I needed to escape, and that time not spent having ecstatic spiritual experiences or pulling others out of *The Matrix* was time wasted on meaningless things. It was a kind of implied gnosticism that I unwittingly assumed was the Christian story. I remember driving past a full movie theater parking lot on my way to my weekly four-hour Saturday night spiritual revival meeting and looking down on all the people wasting their lives on such nonspiritual things. This was my holy act of raging against the machine. Maybe one day they'd come to my prayer meetings and get *red-pilled* too.

The problem was that most of my life was filled with supposedly meaningless, nonspiritual things. I had to work a regular job, take my young kids to the park, go grocery shopping with my wife, and socialize with an entire world of people who were never coming to my prayer meetings. I was depressed with normal life and couldn't integrate the pieces together inside the story I was living in. Even my closest relationships felt like a show about nothing that I needed to escape from.

I can't surf, but one of the things I've heard from surfers is that the waves will always give you feedback on whether you're doing things right. Thankfully, reality gave me feedback that my escapist spirituality wasn't working. I began scanning for an upgrade to my story that could integrate all of it together.

One of the benefits of having invested so much of my young life into Christian spirituality was that I was gradually exposed to time-tested theology and philosophy. The deeper I went, and the more I dug into the wisdom of the past, the more I began to see that gnostic, spiritual escapism was at the heart of my problems.

For Schmemann, the danger in the opposite ditch of spiritual escapism is the tendency to hyperfocus on *activism,* which makes the goal of the whole Story to improve social conditions and make the world "better." The question Schmemann asks is, "Better toward what end?" Without answering the question of what the ultimate purpose of life is beyond just expanding it and trying to keep it from ending, we unwittingly keep building skyscrapers on sand.

This has been an ongoing problem for many of the older mainline churches in America for decades, such as Methodist and Episcopalian churches, which continue to experience a significant decline in numbers, even as the numbers begin to slowly rise in other church contexts. As one mainline leader confessed to me several years ago, "We've gotten stuck thinking our successes in the Civil Rights Movement are what this whole thing is about."

But neither retreating into an escapist spirituality nor exhausting ourselves in a frenzied hustle culture to save the world actually solves our meaning crisis or saves the world. The first question we must answer is, "What is the true nature of life itself?"

Schmemann's answer is the same conclusion Jordan Hall came to after finding the solution to civilizational collapse in a little country church: Communion. If the true Pattern at the core of reality is kenotic love, and if creation itself is given as a good gift for us to steward, then there is no place in all of creation that is meaningless and profane. Living in the Story gives us a sacramental view of the world.

INTERPRETING THE WORLD WITH A SACRAMENTAL LENS

A sacramental view of the world changes a loaf of bread and a cup of wine (or grape juice for all my Baptist friends) into the body and blood of Christ. It sees the material and the spiritual as an integrated whole. This is a way of interpreting the world around us and attending to the moments of our days that transform it from a show about nothing into something good to be received, revered, and offered back to God and others in love.

My friend Andy Squyres is a metamodern poet and songwriter with a special knack for reframing our show about nothing through a sacramental lens. Andy wrote these metamodern, sacramental verses in his 2025 song "Miracle Service," which perfectly captures how our post-cynical mood affords us an opportunity to step into a complex, sometimes brutally hard, but fundamentally sacred world:

> Smog over the valley, snow in the Sierras
> I am heading out of my cynical eras
> Miracle Service every Wednesday night at 6 p.m.
> No time to rehearse this. No strength left to curse this
> Sing the chorus even if you don't know the verses
> God has never done me wrong. Can you say amen?
> Plan for Armageddon. Plant yourself a garden
> Gas in California is six dollars a gallon
> Never mind the future. Turn off your computer
> The side effect of faith is that you get a sense of humor
> Eat a bowl of Froot Loops, take your kids to youth group,
> Hang out with your boys in the summer on the front stoop
> Pray with me and Terry. Call your stepdad, Gary
> Let him off the hook for having dreams that he miscarried.[1]

Andy Squyres taps into the metamodern vibe shift and invites his readers and listeners to reframe the *Seinfeld* moments of their days with a sacramental imagination. His post-ironic sincerity serves as a clarion call to those who have bottomed out on spiritual escapism, activism, and deconstruction alike: Leave the cynicism behind. It's not making you smarter than everyone else, and it's not protecting you from the world; it's just distorting your perception of it. Yes, the world is hard, but how we attend to it changes our experience of it.

Sometimes a singular moment of epiphany can completely reorient us. Some people have profound conversion experiences where it suddenly feels like their attention has been completely rearranged and the world has been instantly transformed through a sacramental lens. Cognitive and behavioral scientists who have studied these experiences refer to this as a *systematic insight*. My friend John Vervaeke's research on systematic insights identified four common features:

1. **CLARITY:** an expansion of vision that simultaneously brings a greater awareness of finite details
2. **BEAUTY:** where the world feels pregnant with wonder and purpose
3. **PEACE:** an enhanced inner sense of connectedness to reality where one feels the different facets of their inner life are working together in mutual harmony
4. **JOY:** a profound sense of energy and vitality; an exciting sense of being "at one" in the very core of their being with reality[2]

When a systematic insight happens, some feel like their entire operating system has been updated. They feel born again. For others, this process of transformation moves at a slower pace. To some extent, which one happens to us is outside our control. How grace comes to us can vary; our responsibility is simply to attend to it.

If we can understand the case made by philosophers like Esther Meek and David Bentley Hart—that how we relate to something changes the way we see it—then we can begin to see that attention is a spiritual act. Training our attention to be rightly oriented toward that which is of ultimate concern is how we move out of our crisis of meaning and into a world filled with invitation for Communion.

RETRAINING OUR ATTENTION

In the Christian tradition, a number of practices exist for responding to the invitations of grace and stepping into the Story more fully. These practices retrain our attention toward that which is of ultimate concern and lead us to the transformative change of a systematic insight, or what the New Testament calls "the fruit of the Spirit." You can see these practices and rituals as ways of building us from the ground up into the Story, changing our attentional operating system, and helping us integrate our whole messy and mundane lives into something significant.

Theologian Richard Foster, who has dedicated his life's work to the study of Christian spirituality, divides these time-tested practices into three categories: inward practices, outward practices, and community practices. The inward practices are the habits we step into individually, such as prayer or meditation. These inward practices change our operating system in such a way that we can rightly attend to that which is of ultimate concern (God) and then rightly order our attention to the world outside of us.

For example, you could consider the practice of prayer as *attention realignment.* Most people are familiar with praying for a problem to be solved in their life or for the health and well-being of a friend. In the case of praying for friends or loved ones, our attention is being realigned from our own egoic concerns toward the needs of others. This kind of prayer comes with the side effect of increasing our emotional and social intelligence as we learn to be attuned to others, rather than ourselves, all the time. But there are other attention realignment forms of prayer that can help us see that we're not in a show about nothing.

The two most central forms of prayer are commonly referred to as contemplation and meditation, and each does something slightly different to our attention. Contemplation is like *attention upscaling.* You could think of it like a telescope that draws your gaze upward and higher to look at the big picture. It expands your attention with a wide-angle lens. In contemplation, we look up and consider the Infinite, seeing awe, wonder, and grandeur as we grasp at a beauty that is beyond human expression.

In this act of attention upscaling, we get a glimpse of the cosmic scale of God's goodness and love. Contemplation is what John does in that cosmic origin story in John 1 when he invites us to contemplate the Logos. Even reading a profound passage of theology or philosophy can become a moment of attention upscaling. The mind-blowing epiphanies that hit you in contemplation sometimes feel like the scene in *Indiana Jones: Raiders of the Lost Ark* when the bad guys look at the ark of the covenant and their faces melt, except in the best possible way.

Meditation is like *attention downscaling*. It is a practice that helps you see how God is present right beneath your nose. You could think of it like a microscope that opens your eyes to a world of wonder and beauty that goes on every moment of every day in the places you do not normally see.

You could practice the Examen prayer developed by Ignatius of Loyola, where every night you look back on your day, mundane moments and all, with an attentive eye to where movements of kenotic love could be seen in the people and events of your day. Long before cognitive scientists heralded the power of paying attention to our breathing to help us escape states of fight or flight, mystics like Ignatius called people to pay attention to their breath as they prayed.

Both attention upscaling and attention downscaling in prayer serve a vital purpose from neurological and psychological standpoints. Our brain's default operating system focuses most of our attention on survival. That's a setting we came out of the womb with. It's a pretty important setting. After all, if we aren't attending to our surroundings while walking through the woods and a venomous snake springs up out of nowhere and kills us, that's not very good.

This default setting can also cause us serious problems, though. With that default setting, each of us also inherits unhealthy personality predispositions and learned behaviors from the cultures we live in, which combine to give us our normative frame for viewing the world. "I'd like to stay alive" is a healthy perspective, but "I'd like to stay alive even at the cost of your life" is a problem. By default, our normative frame appears to be bent in the wrong direction toward the unhealthy use of our attention.

We don't have to work at being selfish, greedy, or vindictive. This stuff just seems to come naturally to us. The ancient, and understandably complicated for those of us with some church baggage, term for this is *sin*. In the Greek of the New Testament, it is *hamartia*—which literally means "missing the mark."[3]

When our normative frame is off, we interpret the world wrongly and attend to things that don't lead to life. The only way to break harmful normative frames is by disrupting them. When I get stuck in a survival frame that has me interpreting the world as a competition for limited resources and status, I get depressed every time I look at my bank account. This makes me attend to strategies for how I can get more money and status.

But what happens when I step into the Story through a practice of contemplation? My attention gets upscaled. I look up at the innumerable stars in the sky and give thanks to Christ who holds it all together. Light traveling from stars millions of light-years away is reaching my eyes after traveling a journey of truly unfathomable scale at a pace of 186,000 miles per second. And a still, small voice whispers through the wonder, "Is it really a problem that you're not a millionaire?"

My bank account hasn't changed, but being reminded of God's grandeur reorients my perspective on the problem. I am reminded of the question that Alexander Schmemann asked: "What is the true nature of life itself?" My attention gets reoriented toward the only true and satisfying answer: "It's Communion."

RESHAPING OUR RELATIONSHIP TO THE WORLD

As Schmemann rightly observed, inward practices shouldn't lead us to a form of spiritual escapism. Genuine salvation saves us from a show about nothing and human civilization going all *Hunger Games* on us (yes, I'm running out of dystopian pop-culture references here). That's why

Richard Foster argues that our inward practices become the foundation for our outward practices.

Practices like prayer reform our hearts and minds through right attention toward God. Outward practices reshape our habits, relationships, and contributions to the world.

Take the outward practice of simplicity, where we consume less and give away more. In this practice, we intentionally choose to confront our normative, survival-oriented frame that bends our attention toward self-preservation at all costs. We consume less, give away more, and break free not just from anxiety about having enough, but also from a lot of useless clutter that demands extra attention to keep up with. The goal of this outward practice is to unify our internal attention and our outward attention toward that which is of ultimate concern.

Counter to the hyperindividualism of our dominant cultural story, living in the Story is not an individualistic choose-your-own-adventure. This is why we shouldn't neglect the centrality of community practices for living in the Story. DIY spiritualities will always fail because we will inevitably fall back into our default survival mode normative frame, and because some community and its culture will shape you with its stories.

Self-authoring isn't just a theoretical failure; it's a practical one, because we all live in relationship to others in the context of a community that always has a culture, a guiding story, and values. We cannot re-story ourselves. That is not how the human brain even works.

Our brains are wired for imitation because we are hardwired to be a social species. We absorb meaning by mirroring those around us. The influential French literary critic and philosopher René Girard called this *memetic desire*. We don't just desire things; we desire what others desire. Our sense of what matters is profoundly social.

We also know from the study of plants, animals, and humans across the world that few things more directly impact the development of all living things than their environment. Take the thorny devil lizard in Australia and the horned lizard in North America. If you looked at them side by side, you would say they are closely related. They both have sharp, protruding spikes covering their heads and bodies. They both have similar coloration and body shape too.

But when scientists compared their DNA and family history, they realized that these two lizards aren't really related at all. In fact, they were about as genetically related as you are to a kangaroo. So, why would they look so similar? It's because they live in similar desert environments, face similar dangers, and eat similar foods that they developed similar features. Their environment shaped who they are.

Obviously, these two different lizards didn't develop the same external features in response to their environment in just one generation, but that doesn't mean that we should overlook what our environment and the people we're surrounded by are doing to us and who we become. Most of us already get that our environments and communities change us on some level. Parents who want their kids to become elite basketball or volleyball players pay top dollar to try to get them on teams with top talent, not just because it might improve their chances of being noticed by a college coach, but because being in that environment with that community shapes them into better athletes.

This is why the Christian story has never been detached from the call to live in Christian community. We can't live in the reality of Communion at the center of it all if we are detached from community. Historically, Christian communities have shared practices and rituals designed to shape our narrative identities in conformity with the Story. These communities will reenact the drama of the Story through practices such as communion, baptism, confession, and worship.

These practices in community have always been essential, but in a culture of hyperindividualism and constant attention farming from our world of screens, we are in even greater need of an anchor in community. These rhythms in community—the praying, singing, serving, forgiving, and feasting—aren't just religious busywork; they're how the Story sinks in and takes hold of our lives. It's how our desires get recalibrated and how the compass of our soul gets reoriented toward true north.

LIFE AS KENOSIS TRAINING

Whether in the context of a neighborhood church or on your commute to work, the various practices that have us stepping into the Story can sometimes produce in us a transcendent experience that goes beyond the wildest psychedelic trip. Other times they are as mundane as waiting for a table at a Chinese restaurant. Which experience we get is often outside of our control. All the great mystics can tell you that. But both have a purpose.

Each is training us to know what love really is and how to live in it forever.

If you've been married for long enough, you understand this. Some days are your anniversary, filled with romance, fine wine, and ecstasy. Other days, you're cleaning poop out of your toddler's butt crack. If your married life lasts long enough, you may even get to change each other's diapers. It's not quite as hot and steamy as when you had bikini bods back on your honeymoon, but that old love is still doing something important in you.

It's conforming you to that kenotic love at the center of it all. It's opening up your character to even deeper Communion.

For some of the earliest Christian theologians, our lives in this world, filled with both joy and sorrow, were intended to be like a hospital for our souls. All that is bent in us, with all of those survival instincts of our normative frame that so often lead to the suffering and death of others, must be healed if the world is to one day be finally set right. Another way of saying this is that our story is all about character development. The more our capacity for living in that kenotic love expands, the less we will attend to things that miss the mark.

If the purpose of the Story is communion, then even the insignificant *Seinfeld* moments have a sacred significance in moving ourselves and the world toward that end. Waiting in traffic affords an opportunity to grow in patience. Grinding at a job that helps care for your family and others but doesn't seem to do much to save the world is still an opportunity to grow in discipline and others-centered love. Cleaning poopy diapers is 100 percent pure kenosis training.

If the point is communion, then everything—yes, even the *Seinfeld* moments—counts. The late-night feeding counts. The traffic jam counts. That awkward conversation with your stepdad, the quiet apology you didn't want to give, the thankless work that no one claps for—each one is a thread in the fabric of who you're becoming.

When your attention has been trained by the rhythms of grace, even the mundane starts to feel sacred. Our show about nothing turns out to be a show about *everything*. With our attention retrained and our desires recalibrated, we don't just see the world differently—we live differently in it. We forgive where we might have raged. We plant where we might have fled. We bless where we might have scorned. We join God not only in perceiving the sacredness of our world, but in participating in its restoration.

The Christian hope is that all these mundane and messy moments—changing diapers, doing dishes, going to church, sitting bedside with a dying loved one—get connected together at the very end of the episode. But it's not for a nihilistic punch line. It's for a climactic culmination. Our story is part of that Story. It's building toward the restoration of everything everywhere.

If this is true, then the sacred can't stay sequestered. Our culture is ready for renewal. Armed with renewed meaning, it is time to renew our sense of calling in the world.

The time to rebuild is now.

CHAPTER 15

Rebuilding During the Apocalypse

> Renewal occurs when people get to the end of themselves, when the social bonds that have kept us strong begin to break, when the stories we have told to explain the world no longer make sense.
>
> *Mark Sayers*

Zombies, ecological collapse, AI overlords, wars, and rumors of wars—our screens are filled with stylized apocalyptic stories of civilizational doom. But apocalyptic stories aren't anything new. The end is always nigh.

Every culture has told cautionary tales about where things are headed if the people don't course-correct. These stories are less about detailed predictions and more about deeper pattern recognition. When the cultural environment feels unstable—when institutions fracture, moral norms erode, and signs of a meaning crisis surround us—our brains begin to sense that an uncertain future is up for grabs.

As we've already seen, this cultural destabilization often sparks a surge of nostalgia. Cue the endless reboots, sequels, and prequels. When the present stories can't hold us together, we look to the past for hints at what once worked. But we don't just look back—we look forward. Behavioral scientists call this "prospective cognition," which is our ability to anticipate, rehearse, and emotionally prepare for possible futures. It's how we map out the prospective trajectory of our current life strategies and figure out what to do now to avoid future ruin.

Apocalyptic stories help us do just that. They terrify, but they also *clarify*. They are like culture-wide exercises in prospective cognition. Zombie hordes and alien invasions may be unrealistic visions of the future, but that's how apocalyptic stories work. It could be a video game like *Fallout*, a film like *28 Years Later*, or the biblical book of Revelation with its imagery of dragons and a white-horse rider with a sword coming out of the rider's mouth. They use fantastical settings and imagery to capture our attention as symbolic stand-ins for our fears of civilizational collapse. What we're really doing with these stories is scanning the cultural landscape for the root problem we must fix to avoid disaster. They are a warning: Live out of alignment with reality, and ruin awaits.

This is why, in the Christian tradition, the word *apocalypse* doesn't mean destruction. It means "unveiling." The Hebrew prophets of the Old Testament weren't just forecasting doom like modern clickbait headlines. They were unveiling the consequences of living out of step with the Pattern that's at the center of it all. When the prophet Jeremiah warned Jerusalem of its impending destruction, he wasn't trying to boost ratings for a dying cable news station. He was trying to clarify the people's vision and call them back into alignment with reality. However, the people didn't see or listen, and the dystopian vision became their reality. In 586 BC, the Babylonians razed Jerusalem and stacked the dead bodies in the nearby Valley of Hinnom to be burned.

Five centuries later, Jesus stood in a rebuilt Jerusalem and issued a similar warning. He told the people that the consequence of going against the grain of God's good ordering was *Gehenna*—a word most Bibles translate as "hell," but which literally referred to that same Valley of Hinnom in his Aramaic tongue. In AD 70 Jerusalem was destroyed again. The fires of Gehenna weren't just a metaphor.

Apocalyptic stories are a wake-up call, not a death sentence. They unveil what has gone wrong and offer a path back to life. That's why the end-of-the-world genre never goes out of style. Every generation is born into a world that is in some state of ruin. Our newest versions may have higher budgets and CGI, but they hint at the same old wisdom. There's a narrow road that leads to life and a wide road that leads to ruin.

But here's the paradox: Even as we continue to binge dystopian stories, something is changing about how we respond to those stories. The nihilism of the 1990s through the 2010s is losing its grip. The irony-soaked detachment that once passed for wisdom is starting to feel like anesthesia, and anesthesia doesn't do you much good if you're free-falling into Gehenna. All the signs that our anti-story was cracking really started to show as we moved into the 2020s. Why?

We got hit with a real apocalypse.

OUR APOCALYPTIC UNVEILING

Whether you interpreted it more like the movie *Contagion* or Orwell's *1984*, the pandemic was an unveiling. It exposed fault lines in our failed guiding stories and the ways in which our way of life isn't rooted in Communion. Civilization's Game A got exposed. Our values were brought to the threshing floor and tossed into the air like wheat as we waited to see what might fall back to earth.

After that, something shifted.

The collective realization began to dawn that all the *seeing through* we had been doing wasn't going to save us. All our cynicism had run its course. When the waves of the pandemic started to wane in 2022, we began to see the vibe shift that David Foster Wallace had longed for all the way back in the 1990s. That new sincerity slowly moved from the margins, where poets and prophets reside, into the mainstream. This was a cultural turn provoked by the apocalyptic realization that our civilization has been on the wide way to doomsday.

You don't get the thunderous success of *Top Gun: Maverick* if it comes out in 2019. The film only lands in 2022 because we had lived through that strange fever-dream apocalypse, where baseball games were played in empty stadiums, funerals were held on Zoom, and people in masks burned our cities with pent-up, anti-story rage. Creed doesn't become a post-ironic icon in 2023 unless something had snapped in us—something that was exhausted with deconstruction and ready for a taste of sincere wholesomeness.

Even the data tells a story. After decades of decline, the rise of the nones began to taper off after our apocalypse. People slowly inched their way back into old church pews. As the saying goes, "There are no atheists in foxholes." And we had just lived through a war of the soul.

Apocalypses aren't really about how things end. They're invitations to begin again.

THE INVITATION TO REBUILD WITHIN THE STORY

This is our moment of invitation. A zeitgeist shift has arrived, and a generational window of opportunity has opened. We can feel it in the increased openness to tradition, the revival of time-tested religious rituals, and the hunger for stories that rebuild what cynicism once dismantled. There is a spiritual ache in the air, and what it reveals is not just the failure of the old guiding stories, but the call to return to the true one.

This is our chance to remember why we were written into the Story in the first place. To be the kind of people who plant, who build, and who bless. Not just to find individual meaning for ourselves, but to rediscover our shared human calling—to preserve the Story, to revitalize the culture, to bless the world. We're called to be *goodmakers.*

In the biblical narrative, humanity is not created merely to escape the world after passing a morality fitness test or a right-belief multiple-choice exam. Our vocational calling is much deeper than that. That's why our place in the Story begins with tending a garden where we walk with God in the cool of the day and ends in a city where God dwells with people of every culture.

Being made in the image of God means that our calling is to *image* God in the world. When God brought reality into existence, he spoke. One of the primary ways we recover our true human vocation and image God in the world is by preserving and telling the Story.

This is why J. R. R. Tolkien called our human vocation "sub-creators."[1] We imitate the Creator by cultivating beauty, truth, and goodness within God's already good world. Whether you do this as a writer like Tolkien, a teacher, an engineer, or a stay-at-home parent, you tell the Story in every creative act of kenotic love.

We must preserve the Story, not like we're guarding a fragile museum relic, but like we're keeping a torch aflame in the night. Without the flame, a culture loses sight of the encroaching darkness. In every generation, the task has been the same: Hold on to the Story, keep it burning, and prevent it from being co-opted.

This is why the ancient Israelites were set apart to preserve the true human vocational calling. They were told to rehearse the Story in feasts, festivals, songs, and scrolls. Even when they were hauled off into exile, a faithful remnant held fast and tended gardens in Babylon. Eventually, the time would come when the failed guiding stories of Babylon would collapse, and faithful leaders like Daniel would be looked to for wisdom on the way forward. An apocalypse in the Babylonian Empire gave way to a Persian Empire, but in the rise and fall of both, Daniel was respected as a visionary. Whenever their world was headed toward ruin, the powerful turned to Daniel for guidance.

This vocational call is picked up by the first followers of Jesus—who were both Jews and Gentiles—and pulled into the family business. These early Christians gathered weekly to retell and reenact the Story through song, scripture, and the breaking of bread together. In doing so, they weren't creating a brand-new culture. They told the Story in Greek, traveled on Roman roads, reasoned with philosophers, and even had showdowns with local magicians (see Acts 8:9–24). They lived in the tension of faithfully preserving and telling the Story without being assimilated into the dominant cultural guiding stories that lead to ruin.

The early Christians refused to bow to Caesar or burn incense to the emperor because they lived under a different King. In doing so, they didn't just say no to Rome—they said yes to a radically different vision of life. The Roman story was steeped in cruelty, with their culture founded on the myth of a murder between twin brothers, Romulus and Remus, who were descendants of the god of war. Romulus killed Remus and founded the city of Rome. In this culture, power was everything and pity was weakness.

Into that culture's guiding story these early Christians carried a Story where God became weak, embraced the lowly, and called his followers to love their enemies and care for the least of them. Over and over, the powers of Rome tried to stomp out this story. Yet, not only did these ancient followers of Jesus' Way persevere and preserve the Story, but their faithful witness transformed Roman culture from within. When the apocalypse came to Rome, and the empire eventually collapsed under the weight of its own decadence and division, the Story remained. It was the bones of that true Story—its ethic, its vision of the human person, its radical mercy—that gave Western civilization a way forward. Even as the lights of that ancient empire dimmed, the flame of the Story was kept burning. Today we universally decry the evils of rape and infanticide, which were cultural norms in that "civilized" society, only because people faithfully preserved the Story.

To live in the Story today is to take up that same calling. In a civilization that we have felt is flirting with collapse, the task isn't to win a culture war or retreat to a safe enclave. It's to keep the fire burning. To know the Story well enough to pass it on. To tell it not just with words, but with the unfolding story of our lives.

The vibe shift we've been tracing gives us a unique opportunity to reconnect with this facet of our vocational calling. After decades of ironic distance and postmodern detachment, people are turning toward what makes them feel wholesome. They're not asking for airtight arguments that win debates; they're searching for a way to live that veers away from Gehenna. This cultural posture creates a rare opening for the Story to be told again—not as a tired pitch or a weapon in the culture war, but as the lifeline it actually is.

PLANTING SUNFLOWERS AT FUKUSHIMA

Poet Joshua Luke Smith is one example of someone fulfilling this vocational calling and showing us what it's like to preserve and tell the Story in our metamodern age. His spoken word poems, which are equal parts apocalyptic warnings and relentless hope, thread the sacred through the ordinary, transforming funerals, fields, and fallout zones into icons of kenotic love. With the poetic sensibility of a psalmist and the fire of a minor prophet, Smith doesn't retreat into sentimentality or cynicism. He names the exile, feels the ache, and still dares to say, "Plant a garden in Babylon." In his poem "Sunflowers in Babylon," Smith announces:

> Did you hear of Fukushima when the sea brewed
> And the earth hurled herself into the ground
> A nuclear site erupted, and an invisible storm rained down
> contaminating the land and poisoning the food,
> And they evacuated thousands
> But for those that couldn't move
> They stayed housed in
> surrounded by elusive clouds that lingered like ghosts
> Becoming suspicious of the air that they once innocently consumed
> And yet amongst the chaos there was a monk dressed in
>   crimson hues
> Who walked through those fields
> planting sunflower seeds within the ruins
> And over time they grew

And they removed the poison
Sunflowers offering themselves as objects of both beauty and
atonement
They drew the cancer from the ground into themselves
until it was broken down
announcing where sunflowers lift their golden crowns
We find evidence of this hope
Even in the soil of decay, something beautiful can grow.[2]

To preserve and tell the Story like ancient Christians in Rome or like Joshua Luke Smith in our increasingly metamodern age, where apocalypse and hope meet, is the necessary foundation for us to fulfill the second facet of our true human calling—revitalizing the culture we inhabit. It's an understandable mistake to see Christianity as a culture, but that's never been what living in The Way is really about. If we look at how the Pattern of patterns has worked throughout time, authentic Christianity doesn't start its own culture from scratch or consume cultures by force. It revitalizes culture from the inside out, reorienting it in all its unique beauty toward true fulfillment. When we step into the Story, we aren't asked to abandon our culture; we are trained to renew it from within. We rewrite the cultural code from below.

Our Christian predecessors rehumanized abandoned infants, built the first hospitals and universities, and created works of outstanding beauty that took generations to complete. Their inward practices, outward practices, and community practices all happened within a preexisting cultural context that radically improved that society. Churches didn't invent pipe organs. Christian mystics weren't the first to tell people to pay attention to their breath as they prayed. They didn't invent medicine. What they did with those cultural tools was redirect their focus to that which is of ultimate concern—God.

When a culture aligns its priorities with what should be of ultimate concern, it begins to rightly order the lesser, but still important, concerns. When this happens, collaborative efforts to save the world really do become heroic. If we know, as Alexander Schmemann asked, what the true purpose of life is, we can set out on adventures to slay dragons and rebuild civilization from the code level up.

I know a couple of different guys named Daniel who are leaders in different Christian communities that remind me what it looks like to step into a Story and revitalize culture. One of them lives not too far from me in Saint Paul, Minnesota. His large church community acquired a dying department store and transformed what would have been an urban eyesore into a place of worship.

With a massive department store parking lot that was going unused most of the week, they partnered with a local nonprofit to build tiny homes on the lot that provided housing for people experiencing homelessness. This cultural renewal project, called Settled, continues to build "sacred settlements" on other church properties, which not only meets the material needs of food and shelter for those in desperate need but also connects them to a community centered on Communion. In that community, people find a connection to the wholesome and learn vital skills that help them break the cycles of crisis that once plagued their lives.

My other friend named Daniel leads a large Christian community in Colorado. Seeing so much of the ruin in their own backyard, the community dreamed of a way to halt the encroaching darkness and despair. They couldn't fix the whole world but knew they were called to start somewhere. So they took an abandoned meth house in their city and built out of its ruins a free healthcare clinic for women and a beautiful apartment complex for single mothers who were victims of abuse, poverty, and abandonment. Mary's Home provides free housing, counseling, skills training, and career prep to women and their children who might otherwise be on a downward trajectory toward ruin.

These are just a few snapshots of what it looks like to recover our true human calling in the world, but these stories are everywhere. Just Google "church erases medical debt" and read story after story of churches around the US that have wiped out millions of dollars of medical debt for people in their community. When a natural disaster devastates a region, like when Hurricane Helene brought catastrophic damage to the American Southeast in 2024, who do you expect to arrive first on the scene for the recovery and rebuild? It ain't the atheism discussion group on Reddit or even the federal government. It's people living in the Story.

This is what it looks like when people work together to embody the Pattern in community. Renewal is the inevitable by-product of living in the Story together. It overflows from the transformation of our inner world. It spills out into neglected places and fills them with meaning. It might start small, like a mustard seed, but it grows into a future that people can live in.

WHY NOW IS THE TIME

To everything there is a season. Especially when the spirit of the age shifts, you should discern what season you're living in if you want to bear fruit. What makes for good work depends on the season. Planting seeds in the spring is good work. Planting them in the winter is not, even though the work looks the same. And as we've seen throughout this book, the cultural seasons are changing.

Maybe this is just a flash-in-the-pan moment. Maybe we revert back to the anti-story and once again lock ourselves inside our cynical prisons. It's not impossible, but here's one reason why I think that's unlikely.

The year 2030.

Is that the year of some important presidential election or global AI tech conference? No. That's the year the last of the Baby Boomers will have reached the typical retirement age of sixty-five. A generational sea change in institutional leadership will unfold over the next several years as CEOs, executive leaders, pastors, and lifelong politicians move into retirement.

Boomers hold a disproportionate share of senior leadership roles, and an estimated ten thousand of them head into retirement every day. In the public sector, many are talking about a "gray tsunami" where Boomers are retiring faster than their roles can be filled. In the private and non-profit sectors, major succession challenges abound as many Boomer leaders, who valued large power distances between themselves and their subordinates, now struggle with identifying capable young leaders to move to the head of the table after they are gone. But someone must fill these leadership vacancies.

Gen Xers, Millennials, and older Zoomers can't afford to carry on with anti-story values or rail against the system when they are now the ones being entrusted to carry the mantles of leadership. Aspirational vision, hope, and sincerity will be functional necessities as we are thrust into these positions of leadership. Men and women of character and moral fortitude *must* lead the way.

It was easy to cynically tear down and deconstruct when we didn't feel like we had a seat at the table, but those seats are now opening up. What kind of world do we want our children and grandchildren to inherit? We must rebuild within the Story that has Communion at the center.

This pivot from expressing anti-establishment angst to assuming responsibility for the institutions that support and preserve civilization is the core message at the heart of the latest iteration of another great American mythological hero: *Batman*. In the 2022 version of the Caped Crusader, we meet the most vengeful, disillusioned, and depressed of the big-screen Dark Knights. Some cultural commentators called him the Batman for the "incel" generation (an internet term referring to men who are involuntarily celibate and terminally online).

In the climactic resolution of the film, this Batman realizes that all his cynicism and vengeance, which drove him to act outside of the system, would not save the city he loved so dearly. Even though he deeply cared for Gotham, his rogue actions inspired other rogue actors who were willing to tear a corrupt society down at all costs. Instead of vengeance, the young vigilante hero realizes he must be driven by hope instead and become a willing partner with institutions for lasting change to be possible.

In the penultimate scene, Batman carries an illuminating torch through the wreckage of deconstruction, leading in his trail a host of government leaders and civil servants who must now cooperate to rebuild the city and its institutions together in its next chapter. In his closing monologue, as he helps to care for the wounded, the young Dark Knight shows his change in perspective:

> Vengeance won't change the past—mine or anyone else's. I have to become more. People need hope. To know someone's out there for them. This city's angry, scared. Like me. Our scars can destroy us, even after the physical wounds have healed. But if we can survive them, they can transform us. They can give us the power to endure . . . And the strength to fight.[3]

Why must we carry with us sincerity, hope, and a longing for the wholesome? Why must we reject the antivision appeal to destroy our institutions? Because now is the time to carry them forward, to reform where there has been corruption or ineptitude, and to rebuild where there has been ruin.

Yes, there is a prophetic call to *see through* corruption and to tear down idols that is supported within the Story, but to everything there is a season—and not every season is a Jeremiah season. Sometimes being a prophet looks like Nehemiah's example.

Nehemiah was an Old Testament prophet charged not with shouting at a crumbling system on the verge of collapse from outside it, but with being a builder embedded within it. With Jerusalem in ruins long after the destruction Jeremiah had foretold came true, Nehemiah was charged with the task of rebuilding the walls of the city—but it wasn't just a physical construction he led. Nehemiah led a spiritual reconstruction in a post-apocalyptic world. In just fifty-two days, the people rebuilt the walls together and were united in the shared story read by Ezra the Scribe.

After living in exile for so long, the people had lost sight of the Story.

Rebuilding and reeducating went hand in hand. Cultural renewal was, and always is, inseparable from spiritual renewal.

Now is a season for rebuilding.

If you're reading this as a Baby Boomer or older you might be wondering, "Where do I fit in this season? Should I just retire to a beach and leave the younger generations alone?"

Absolutely not. Get some beach time and pickleball in, but the younger generations still need you.

Maybe you got used to the rage-against-the-machine years, where people mocked your white New Balance shoes and your "try-hard" sincerity as cringe, and you've been reluctant to reach out to younger generations to offer support and encouragement or an invitation to mentorship. Well, I've got good news for you. Those twentysomethings are rocking your New Balances now, and a growing number of them aren't running away from the traditional wisdom you have to offer.

One couple in their sixties recently told me of the unexpected surprise it's been for them to invite young couples they meet at church to their home and not only have them say yes, but to have them come over, eat up every story and nugget of wisdom the older couple offers, and then refuse to leave when the hosts are ready for their regular 9 p.m. bedtime.

People of every generation, remember that wholesome is the new cynicism. Don't be afraid to pursue the wholesome at the cost of cringe. Embrace the cringe.

When my friend John Mark McMillan decided to bring his teenage son on his rock-and-roll tour to play as a member of the band this past year, he was a little worried that people might see that as cringe. Father-son duos don't exactly scream rock and roll. Instead, he found that everyone he talked to at the show was inspired by how wholesome it was. If broken families became the status quo in our anti-story age, then maybe a dad and his son with their guitars in hand is rock and roll.

In the previous cultural season, calling out plastic spirituality was en vogue. No one wants to be duped by pseudo-meaning, even if it's wearing church clothes. But we're in a planting and growing season, so don't frame your mission as being the antihero who sees through everything. There's a season for *seeing through*, but this isn't that season.

Just grow something beautiful instead. Start a company or nonprofit that makes something good in the world. Dream with your community about how to build something that intercepts someone's collision course with Armageddon.

One of the best pieces of advice I ever received from a respected mentor came as I was figuring out how to navigate my role at an event with multiple guest speakers presenting viewpoints I believed were destructive. I knew he had been in situations like this before and wondered how he did it. He told me, "Paul, instead of trying to tear down everything that's false, I just try to add something true to the conversation. I trust the truth can stand on its own and do the work."

Outrage is the default currency of our social media landscape. It's the easiest way to trick our survival instincts into giving a social post or news article our attention. But we've been so saturated in outrage that it's becoming white noise. I mean, we all lived through an apocalypse already, so take down the Chicken Little act a few notches, everyone. You can spend your days perpetually outraged, swinging wildly at all that is false in the world, or you can add something true to the conversation and let it stand on its own.

We don't need to be what David Foster Wallace called "Third World rebels" anymore. According to Wallace, "Third World rebels are great at exposing and overthrowing corrupt, hypocritical regimes, but they seem noticeably less great at the mundane, non-negative task of then establishing a superior governing alternative."[4]

The vibe shift is a calling to establish a superior governing alternative.

Bear witness to the Story. Tend a garden even if you're in Babylon. What's broken will inevitably fall on its own. If it doesn't adhere to the Pattern, it always unravels. Drop the antivisions, the anti-stories, and the talk of being a revolutionary. Go build something instead. Learn to care for a place. Maybe even collaborate on a project that doesn't get completed in your lifetime.

Celebrate what's true, good, and beautiful all around you. Be ambitious again. Don't be the vain kind of ambitious that builds monuments to your own ego. Be the kind of ambitious that looks at an abandoned meth house and says, "Now *that* I can work with!" Dream of curing diseases. Dream of raising good children. Work hard so you can bless the world even more with your talents and abilities.

Live as if the Story is true—because it is. Your life will be filled with meaning, and you will recover a sense of mission in the world. Together we can pull our culture out of the orbit of the anti-story and rebuild out of the ruins.

It's time to rebuild.

Acknowledgments

I've been writing and speaking about the ideas in this book for many years, but I noticed a significant spike in broader interest in my work in 2024. This coincided with one of the more difficult stretches for my family that I can recall. A mysterious set of ailments for a family member and a quest to find solutions became an all consuming endeavor for my wife and me, along with our three children.

In the fall of 2024, I had a passing conversation with my wife in which I told her, "When we get out of this swirl, I think I might have a book to write." With no clear end in sight to our "locust years," I put the idea on the shelf in some back corner of my mind along with a mental note—a note that may have even risen to some form of wistful prayer—about who my dream editor and publisher would be.

On the night of my birthday in late November of 2024, I received an email from someone with the question, "Have you considered writing a book about the things you've been talking about lately?" It was from that exact "dream editor" I had taken a mental note of and prayed some half-hearted prayer for just a few weeks earlier. It seemed as if the time to write this book, which is really all about hope, wasn't going to be when all the conditions seemed perfect. How ironic. The time to do it was now.

That began a process of dialogue with the illustrious Paul J. Pastor (executive editor at HarperCollins/Nelson Books, author of *The Locust Years*, and the dream editor I'd always wanted to work with) and the wonderful people at Nelson Books, spearheaded by my fantastic literary agent Keely Boeving at WordServe Literary Group.

Thank you for seeing that this book needed to be made and for creating a path for me to share it with so many. I've been continually reminded throughout this process that all of this is a gift that I didn't scrap and claw to get. I mean, I didn't even offer a very good prayer to work with Paul Pastor and Nelson. It's all been grace.

Eight years of podcasting, where I processed aloud with many of the people mentioned in this book, were foundational to the formation of *Based on a True Story*. The dialogue partners are too many to list here, and I'm also afraid I might inadvertently neglect some in trying to list them all, but each of you who've participated in my podcast were invaluable partners in the creation of this book. That work could not have continued without a number of patrons either, who also became dialogue partners through forums, Discord server discussions, and group Zoom calls. You, too, have a share in the creation of this book and deserve my deepest thanks.

I'm also indelibly grateful to my church community at First Free over these past eight years. Among the many ways you have supported me, one of the most practically beneficial ways was the sabbatical you blessed me with in the summer of 2024. That afforded me the opportunity to create some timeless memories with my wife and children, but it also gave me the space to immerse myself in the theological and spiritual formation literature that would come to shape the important closing chapters of this book (though I did not know I'd even be writing a book at that time).

Andy Squyres, John Mark McMillan, and Joshua Luke Smith—thank you, brothers, for graciously allowing me to incorporate extensive sections of your lyrics and poetry into this book. You made this book exponentially better, and I hope people who read this spend a ton of money on your records, books, and tours.

My ability to navigate the intersection of religion, philosophy, and science has benefitted tremendously from the collaborative research and writing projects over the last several years with Clay Routledge at Archbridge Institute's Human Flourishing Lab. Clay's research is mentioned on several occasions in this book, and for good reason. It's brilliant. He, along with John Vervaeke at the University of Toronto, have been instrumental in processing with me, as two of North America's leading experts, the cognitive and behavioral science side of the meaning crisis.

Finally, to Keri, Justice, Autumn, and Ryder, you are the most important people in my story.

Notes

PROLOGUE

1. Robert P. Jones, "Exodus: Why Americans Are Leaving Religion—and Why They're Unlikely to Come Back," PRRI, September 22, 2016, https://prri.org/research/prri-rns-poll-nones-atheist-leaving-religion/.
2. "How U.S. Religious Composition Has Changed in Recent Decades," Pew Research Center, September 13, 2022, https://www.pewresearch.org/?p=70301.
3. Michael Davern et al., *The General Social Survey*, NORC at the University of Chicago, accessed January 26, 2026, https://www.norc.org/research/projects/gss.html; "Religious 'Nones' in America: Who They Are and What They Believe," Pew Research Center, January 24, 2024, https://www.pewresearch.org/?p=69466.
4. Holly Hedegaard et al., "Increase in Suicide Mortality in the United States, 1999–2018," *NCHS Data Brief*, no. 362, Centers for Disease Control and Prevention, April 2020, https://www.cdc.gov/nchs/products/databriefs/db362.htm.
5. "Suicides by Drug Overdose Increased Among Young People, Elderly People, and Black Women, Despite Overall Downward Trend," National Institutes of Health, February 2, 2022, https://www.nih.gov/news-events/news-releases/suicides-drug-overdose-increased-among-young-people-elderly-people-black-women-despite-overall-downward-tren.
6. Jeffrey M. Jones, "U.S. Church Membership Falls Below Majority for the First Time," Gallup, March 29, 2021, https://news.gallup.com/poll/341963/church-membership-falls-below-majority-first-time.aspx;

"Public Trust in Government: 1958–2025," Pew Research Center, December 1, 2025, https://www.pewresearch.org/politics/2025/12/04/public-trust-in-government-1958-2025/; "Five Key Insights Into Americans' Views of the News Media," Gallup, February 27, 2025, https://news.gallup.com/opinion/gallup/657239/five-key-insights-americans-views-news-media.aspx.
7. Barna Group, "New Barna Data: Young Adults Lead a Resurgence in Church Attendance," Barna Group, September 2, 2025, https://www.barna.com/research/young-adults-lead-resurgence-in-church-attendance/.
8. Josh Kristianto, "'I Think Gen Z Is Looking for Meaning': New Data Shows Gen Z Men Returning to Church," ABC15 Arizona, September 30, 2025, https://www.abc15.com/news/local-news/i-think-gen-z-is-looking-for-meaning-new-data-shows-gen-z-men-returning-to-church.

CHAPTER 1: BREAK STUFF: A CULTURE IN COLLAPSE

1. *The Matrix*, directed by the Wachowskis, Warner Brothers, 1999.
2. Francis Fukuyama, *The End of History and the Last Man* (Free Press, 1992).
3. David Foster Wallace, "E Unibus Pluram: Television and U.S. Fiction," in *A Supposedly Fun Thing I'll Never Do Again: Essays and Arguments* (Little, Brown, 1997), 49–97.
4. David Foster Wallace, "Commencement Address," Kenyon College Commencement, May 21, 2005, Gambier, Ohio.
5. Note: It's obvious that countless movies, fiction, TV shows, and comic books are produced with myriad and often contradictory values portrayed. Not all carry the same cultural influence or affect how someone attempts to make sense of the world and their own story. Pop culture influence isn't just this top-down pressure where Hollywood forces people into a theater. It is just as much a bottom-up selection process where tickets purchased, books sold, and even memes shared all shape which stories go on to have powerful, culture-wide influence. There is a fascinating interplay between the "spirit of the age" and not just what stories get made but what stories get culturally *selected* in the market and then carry formative influence.
6. The Pixies, "Where Is My Mind?," track 7 on *Surfer Rosa*, Downtown Recorders, 1988.

CHAPTER 2: YOU LIVE IN A STORY, AND A STORY LIVES IN YOU

1. Vanessa Boris, "What Makes Storytelling So Effective For Learning?" Harvard Business Impact, December 20, 2017, https://www.harvardbusiness.org/insight/what-makes-storytelling-so-effective-for-learning/.
2. Boris, "What Makes Storytelling So Effective?"
3. John Vervaeke, "God, Religion, Ghosts in the Brain & What Happens When We Die," posted December 19, 2025, by Danny Jones, YouTube, www.youtube.com/watch?v=X9ShiRDhvUI.
4. William Grassie, "Entangled Narratives," Metanexus, August 9, 2011, https://metanexus.net/entangled-narratives/.
5. Christian Smith, *Moral, Believing Animals: Human Personhood and Culture* (Oxford University Press, 2003), 64, emphasis added.
6. David Straughan, "Mean World Syndrome: Public Perception of Crime Doesn't Match Reality," Interrogating Justice, July 5, 2021, https://interrogatingjustice.org/decriminalizing-mental-illness/mean-world-syndrome/.
7. Stanley J. Grenz, *Theology for the Community of God* (Eerdmans, 2000), 131.
8. Frank Martela and Michael F. Steger, "The Three Meanings of Meaning in Life: Distinguishing Coherence, Purpose, and Significance," *The Journal of Positive Psychology* 11, no. 5 (2016): 531.
9. Richard Dawkins, *River Out of Eden: A Darwinian View of Life* (Basic Books, 1996), 133.
10. Becka A. Alper et al., "Spirituality Among Americans," Pew Research Center, December 7, 2023, https://www.pewresearch.org/religion/2023/12/07/spirituality-among-americans/.
11. David Crary, "How Many Americans Believe in Astrology and Rely on Fortune-Telling? A New Survey Has Answers," AP News, May 21, 2025, https://apnews.com/article/astrology-tarot-fortune-telling-psychics-41a815371e107ddef503910eaa9d8378.
12. Joshua A. Wilt et al., "Yearning for Something More: Inductive Thematic Analysis of Spiritual Yearning," *The International Journal for the Psychology of Religion* 36, no. 1 (2025): 1–20, https://doi.org/10.1080/10508619.2025.2505355.
13. When it comes to scale and influence, these guiding stories are way

bigger than "The Three Little Pigs." In fact, "The Three Little Pigs" might be considered an effective "henchman" guiding story that works for a much bigger "final boss" guiding story like the Modern Story and gets created, preserved, and passed on to transmit core values and life strategies found in that "final boss" guiding story.

CHAPTER 3: THE MODERN STORY

1. René Descartes, *Meditations on First Philosophy: With Selections from the Objections and Replies*, rev. ed., trans. John Cottingham (Cambridge University Press, 1996).
2. *Star Wars: Episode IV—A New Hope*, directed by George Lucas (Lucasfilm, 1977).
3. *Nacho Libre*, directed by Jared Hess (Paramount Pictures, 2006).
4. Andrew Root, *The Pastor in a Secular Age: Ministry to People Who No Longer Need a God* (Baker Academic, 2019), xviii.
5. Daniel Kahneman and Angus Deaton, "High Income Improves Evaluation of Life but Not Emotional Well-Being," *Proceedings of the National Academy of Sciences* 107, no. 38 (2010): 16489–93, https://doi.org/10.1073/pnas.1011492107; Matthew A. Killingsworth, "Experienced Well-Being Rises with Income, Even Above $75,000 Per Year," *Proceedings of the National Academy of Sciences* 118, no. 4 (2021): e2016976118, https://doi.org/10.1073/pnas.2016976118.
6. Talking Heads, "Once in a Lifetime," *Remain in Light*, Sire, 1980.

CHAPTER 4: THE POSTMODERN ANTI-STORY

1. Friedrich Nietzsche, *Beyond Good and Evil*, trans. Walter Kaufmann (Vintage Books, 1989).
2. The quote is a common clarification of the original: "'There are only facts'—I would say: No, facts is precisely what there is not, only interpretations." Friedrich Nietzsche, *The Will to Power*, trans. Walter Kaufmann and R. J. Hollingdale (Vintage Books, 1968), 267.
3. Yes, I saw *Knives Out 3: Wake Up Dead Man* on Netflix. It came out as this book was going through the editing process. Yes, Father Jud doesn't fit this stereotype, but the other priest, Monsignor Wicks, certainly does.
4. "How U.S. Religious Composition Has Changed in Recent Decades,"

Pew Research Center, September 13, 2022, https://www.pewresearch.org/?p=70301.

5. Theologian Robert K. Johnson observed in *Reel Spirituality: Theology and Film in Dialogue* (Baker Academic, 2006) that one could see a statistical correlation between the rise of home video stores like Blockbuster Video and the decline of church attendance in America. As the theory goes, church was the place that most people in America came to in hopes of finding a true story that could direct the story of their own lives. But the local pastor could not compete with the immersive experience of sight and sound in motion pictures brought straight into our living rooms. It's an interesting theory that, when combined with an understanding of how postmodernism was exploding in pop culture around the same time, helps to make even more sense of a possible cause of rapid church decline.

CHAPTER 5: THE DEATH OF SUPERMAN

1. John Vervaeke, "After Socrates: Episode 2—Socrates, the Monstrous," posted January 9, 2023, by John Vervaeke, YouTube, https://www.youtube.com/watch?v=erxLwlk6RCQ.
2. Ian Harber, *Walking Through Deconstruction: How to Be a Companion in a Crisis of Faith* (InterVarsity Press, 2025).
3. *Batman v Superman: Dawn of Justice*, directed by Zack Snyder, featuring Ben Affleck, Henry Cavill, and Jesse Eisenberg, Warner Bros. Pictures, 2016.
4. Linda Hutcheon, "Gone Forever, But Here to Stay: The Legacy of the Postmodern," in *Supplanting the Postmodern: An Anthology of Writings on the Arts and Culture of the Early 21st Century*, eds. David Rudrum and Nicholas Stavris (Bloomsbury Academic, 2015), 10.
5. Augustine, *The City of God*, trans. Henry Bettenson (Penguin Books, 2003), book XII, chap. 6; Gregory of Nyssa, *The Great Catechism*, trans. William Moore and Henry Austin Wilson, in *Nicene and Post-Nicene Fathers*, Second Series, vol. 5, eds. Philip Schaff and Henry Wace (Christian Literature Publishing, 1893), archived at New Advent, ed. Kevin Knight, www.newadvent.org/fathers/29082.htm; C. S. Lewis, *Mere Christianity* (1952; repr., HarperCollins, 2001).
6. C. S. Lewis, *The Abolition of Man* (1943; repr., HarperOne, 2001), 81.

7. David Foster Wallace, "E Unibus Pluram: Television and U.S. Fiction," *The Review of Contemporary Fiction* (1993), 183, archived at The Free Library, accessed April 15, 2025, https://www.thefreelibrary.com/E+unibus+pluram%3A+television+and+U.S.+fiction.-a013952319.
8. Paul Anleitner (@PaulAnleitner), "Can you feel it? The culture is shifting from cynical to aspirational," X, December 1, 2024, https://x.com/PaulAnleitner/status/1863321980990038374?s=20.
9. Paul Anleitner (@PaulAnleitner), "2. Superman Calls Us Out of Postmodern Cynicism. Postmodernism, with its constant cynicism and irony, is increasingly passé. We're ready for hope and sincerity," X, December 31, 2024, https://x.com/PaulAnleitner/status/1874246596084588819?s=20.
10. *Superman*, directed by James Gunn, DC Studios / Warner Bros. Pictures, 2025.

CHAPTER 6: EVERYTHING EVERYWHERE

1. *Everything Everywhere All at Once*, directed by Daniel Kwan and Daniel Scheinert, A24, 2022.
2. *Deadpool 2*, directed by David Leitch, 20th Century Fox, 2018.

CHAPTER 7: CAN YOU TAKE ME HIGHER?

1. Dan Solomon, "How the Texas Rangers Taught Me to Stop Worrying and Love Creed," *Texas Monthly*, October 27, 2023, https://www.texasmonthly.com/arts-entertainment/texas-rangers-world-series-run-taught-me-creed-slaps/.
2. Solomon, "How the Texas Rangers Taught Me to Stop Worrying."
3. James K. A. Smith, *You Are What You Love: The Spiritual Power of Habit* (Brazos Press, 2016), vii.
4. John Mark McMillan (@johnmarkmcmillan), "But, yeah I'd pretty much quit," Instagram, March 27, 2025, https://www.instagram.com/p/DHtSalMuh8t/?img_index=10.
5. 1 Corinthians 1:27–28.

CHAPTER 8: THIS IS WHAT MOVIES USED TO FEEL LIKE

1. *F1: The Movie*, directed by Joseph Kosinski, Warner Bros. Pictures, 2025.
2. Clay Routledge, *Nostalgia: A Psychological Resource* (Routledge, 2015).

3. Deborah Houlding, "The Greek Philosophers," *The Traditional Astrologer* (January 2000).

CHAPTER 9: CAN A LITTLE COUNTRY CHURCH SAVE THE WORLD?

1. Jordan Hall, recorded interview with author, March 31, 2025.
2. Hall, interview with author.
3. Hall, interview with author.
4. Hall, interview with author.
5. Hall, interview with author.
6. 1 John 4:8b, 12, 16b–19.
7. "Born from Love," by John Mark and Sarah McMillan, used with permission.

CHAPTER 10: HAUNTED BY MAGIC

1. Charles Taylor, *A Secular Age* (Belknap Press, 2007).
2. James K. A. Smith, *How (Not) to Be Secular: Reading Charles Taylor* (Eerdmans, 2014), 3.
3. *Interstellar*, directed by Christopher Nolan, Paramount Pictures / Warner Bros. Pictures, 2014.
4. Clay Routledge, "The Spiritual Species," *National Affairs* (Summer 2020), https://nationalaffairs.com/publications/detail/the-spiritual-species.
5. Jonathan Haidt, *The Righteous Mind: Why Good People Are Divided by Politics and Religion* (Pantheon Books, 2012), 287.
6. Iain McGilchrist, *The Master and His Emissary: The Divided Brain and the Making of the Western World* (Yale University Press, 2019).
7. McGilchrist, *Master and His Emissary*.
8. John Vervaeke, "Awakening from the Meaning Crisis," YouTube playlist, accessed January 27, 2026, https://www.youtube.com/playlist?list=PLND1JCRq8Vuh3f0P5qjrSdb5eC1ZfZwWJ.
9. Vervaeke, "Awakening from the Meaning Crisis."
10. Nicholas Capaldi, "Does Postmodernism Pit Us Against Each Other?," Foundation for Economic Education, July 7, 2017, https://fee.org/articles/does-postmodernism-pit-us-against-each-other/.
11. Becky A. Alper et al., *Spirituality Among Americans*, Pew Research

Center, December 7, 2023, https://www.pewresearch.org/wp-content/uploads/sites/20/2023/12/PR_2023.12.7_spirituality_REPORT.pdf.

CHAPTER 11: DARK MAGIC

1. Christian Smith and Melinda Lundquist Denton, *Soul Searching: The Religious and Spiritual Lives of American Teenagers* (Oxford University Press, 2005), 118.
2. Søren Kierkegaard, *The Sickness Unto Death: A Christian Psychological Exposition for Upbuilding and Awakening*, trans. Howard V. Hong and Edna H. Hong (Princeton University Press, 1980).
3. Ashley Lande, *The Thing That Would Make Everything Okay Forever: Transcendence, Psychedelics, and Jesus Christ* (Lexham Press, 2024), 83.
4. Lande, *Thing That Would Make Everything Okay Forever*, xvi.
5. Lande, *Thing That Would Make Everything Okay Forever*, xvii.
6. Søren Kierkegaard, *Provocations: Spiritual Writings of Søren Kierkegaard*, ed. Charles E. Moore (Plough Publishing House, 1999), 136–41.
7. Kathryn A. MacLean, Matthew W. Johnson, and Roland R. Griffiths, "Mystical Experiences Occasioned by the Hallucinogen Psilocybin Lead to Increases in the Personality Domain of Openness," *Journal of Psychopharmacology* 25, no. 11 (2011): 1453–61, https:/doi.org/10.1177/0269881111420188.
8. Christine Rouselle, "Number of Americans Who Say They Are Witches Is on the Rise," *National Catholic Register*, October 29, 2018, https://www.ncregister.com/news/number-of-americans-who-say-they-are-witches-is-on-the-rise?utm_source=chatgpt.com.
9. Brandon Vogt, "The Return of Paganism," posted January 28, 2019, by Bishop Robert Barron, YouTube, https://www.youtube.com/watch?v=nPM_QhM_a5g.

CHAPTER 12: RELIGIOUS RENAISSANCE

1. Paul Kingsnorth, "The Cross and the Machine," Paul Kingsnorth, accessed January 28, 2026, https://www.paulkingsnorth.net/cross.
2. Kingsnorth, "The Cross and the Machine."
3. Kingsnorth, "The Cross and the Machine."
4. "Rowan Williams & Paul Kingsnorth: Conversion, Culture, and the

Cross," posted June 3, 2022, by Premier Unbelievable?, YouTube, https://www.youtube.com/watch?v=iCxznkRKa1w.

5. Celia Buchanan, "Famed Atheist Richard Dawkins Declares Himself a 'Cultural Christian,'" Beliefnet, March 31, 2024, https://www.beliefnet.com/columnists/news/2024/04/famous-atheist-richard-dawkins-declares-himself-a-cultural-christian.
6. Jonathan Pageau, "The Perfect Mode of Being | Jonathan Pageau | EP 156," posted March 1, 2021, by Jordan B. Peterson, YouTube, https://www.youtube.com/watch?v=2rAqVmZwqZM.
7. Paul Anleitner (@PaulAnleitner), "The vibe shift is hitting University of Oxford," X, May 14, 2025, https://x.com/PaulAnleitner/status/1922670151389835276.
8. Ruth Graham, "In a First Among Christians, Young Men Are More Religious Than Young Women," *New York Times*, September 23, 2024, https://www.nytimes.com/2024/09/23/us/young-men-religion-gen-z.html.
9. Justin Brierley, "The Surprising Truth About the West's Christian Revival," *Think Faith with Justin Brierley*, February 4, 2025, https://justinbrierley.beehiiv.com/p/the-surprising-truth-about-the-west-s-christian-revival.
10. *The Quiet Revival One Year On: What's the Story?* (Bible Society, 2026), PDF, accessed April 13, 2026, https://bible-society.directus.app/assets/4e08929c-6148-49f6-9269-757f6ba3d87d. Just before this book went to the printer, critical reevaluations of this particular study were published. While the quantitative data from this research is being reassessed, we have decided to include it with this note as an approximate distillation of the numerous personal anecdotes and qualitative research that point to a real shift in church attendance among young people in the UK.
11. Glen Scrivener, "Glen Scrivener: Why Christianity Made Us Believe in Kindness, Equality & Progress," posted November 8, 2023, by Seen & Unseen, YouTube, https://www.youtube.com/watch?v=pGtpUpI0_90.
12. Jeffrey A. Trachtenberg, "Sales of Bibles Are Booming, Fueled by First-Time Buyers and New Versions," *The Wall Street Journal*, December 1, 2024, https://www.wsj.com/business/media/sales-of-bibles-are-booming-fueled-by-first-time-buyers-and-new-versions-d402460e.

13. "The State of Church Attendance: Trends and Statistics [2025]," ChurchTrac, accessed January 28, 2026, https://www.churchtrac.com/articles/the-state-of-church-attendance-trends-and-statistics-2023.
14. Matthew Namee et al., *Converts to Orthodoxy: Statistics and Trends from the Past Decade* (Orthodox Studies Institute, Saint Constantine College, 2024), https://resources.finalsite.net/images/v1721762028/saintconstantineorg/fxh1s6pimhcz1meytbyg/convertstudy1_final.pdf.
15. Peter Johnston, "The New Trend of Anglican Growth," *Anglican Compass*, June 27, 2024, https://anglicancompass.com/the-new-trend-of-anglican-growth/.
16. There have been notable voices who have said over the past couple years, and I paraphrase, "Pump the brakes on this talk of massive Christian revival! The national survey data in the US doesn't show significant enough spikes in religious affiliation to warrant that kind of language." What the data does show is a multiyear halt on the rise of nones—a rise that continued upward, essentially unfettered, since the early 1990s and peaked at 32 percent of adults in 2022. The Cooperative Election Study found upward of 35 percent in 2022. Not only has that upward trajectory halted, but we've seen a 4 percent decline in nones since 2022 (as of late 2025 when this book was edited). This, along with the other data I've already referenced, points to something happening that hasn't happened in decades. The closedness is giving way to a state of increasing openness. Is it revival? That's a messy word, which is why I prefer *Religious Renaissance* in this book. My argument is that these conversion stories from cultural tastemakers like Paul Kingsnorth are the front side of a cultural bell curve. I would expect more to follow in the coming years, especially among higher-profile people of cultural influence. The felt vibe shift is a real cultural phenomenon, and the purpose of this book is about the cultural moment, not specifically about whether churches across America are more full than they were ten years ago. Quantitative research like national surveys is just one component of good sociological digging. The 2016 and 2024 US presidential elections should remind us that polling data is not an infallible, objective picture of reality. Qualitative research, like people's stories or even informal anecdotes of pastors seeing higher attendance in their churches or reporting a changing attitude toward religious conversations, shouldn't

be discarded. I suspect that in the next five years, unless some global catastrophe strikes, we will see more significant changes in data that reflect what's rumbling on the front side of the bell curve today.

CHAPTER 13: BASED ON A TRUE STORY

1. John 1:1–5.
2. Heraclitus, *Fragments*, trans. Brooks Haxton (Viking, 2001); Antonia Tripolitis, *Religions of the Hellenistic-Roman Age* (Eerdmans Publishing, 2001), 37–38; Philo, *De Profugis*, cited in Gerald Friedlander, *Hellenism and Christianity* (P. Vallentine, 1912), 114–15.
3. Matthew 14:27.
4. Matthew 14:28–29.
5. C. S. Lewis, "Meditation in a Toolshed," in *God in the Dock: Essays on Theology and Ethics*, ed. Walter Hooper (William B. Eerdmans, 1970).
6. Esther Lightcap Meek, *Loving to Know: Introducing Covenant Epistemology* (Cascade Books, 2011).
7. "U.S. Video Consumption Tops 43 Hours Per Week," Parks Associates, April 17, 2024, https://www.parksassociates.com/blogs/in-the-news/us-video-consumption-tops-43-hours-per-week.
8. "Information," Etymonline, accessed January 28, 2026, https://www.etymonline.com/word/information.
9. Søren Kierkegaard, *Kierkegaard's Journals and Notebooks*, vol. 1, *Journals AA–DD*, eds. Niels Jørgen Cappelørn et al. (Princeton University Press, 2007), 19.

CHAPTER 14: DID YOU EVER NOTICE?

1. Andy Squyres, "Miracle Service," 2025. Used by permission.
2. John Vervaeke, "Ep 11 - Awakening from the Meaning Crisis - Higher States of Consciousness, Part 1," posted March 29, 2019, by John Vervaeke, YouTube, https://www.youtube.com/watch?v=39NpjQDtqNw.
3. "Hamartia," Etymonline, accessed January 28, 2026, https://www.etymonline.com/word/hamartia.

CHAPTER 15: REBUILDING DURING THE APOCALYPSE

1. J. R. R. Tolkien, "On Fairy-Stories," in *The Monsters and the Critics, and Other Essays*, ed. Christopher Tolkien (Houghton Mifflin, 1984), 122.

2. Joshua Luke Smith, "Sunflowers in Babylon." Used by permission.
3. *The Batman*, directed by Matt Reeves, Warner Bros. Pictures, 2022.
4. David Foster Wallace, "E Unibus Pluram: Television and U.S. Fiction," in *A Supposedly Fun Thing I'll Never Do Again: Essays and Arguments* (Little, Brown, 1997).

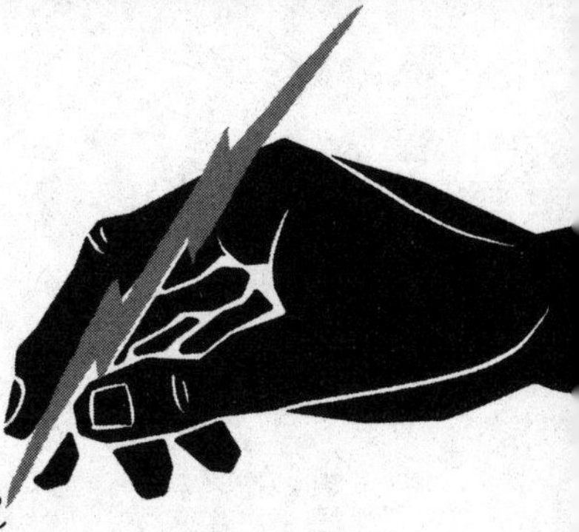

About the Author

Paul Anleitner is a cultural theologian who writes and speaks on the role of culture and story in our quest for meaning. His unique interdisciplinary approach integrates theology, philosophy, and science to help individuals and institutions navigate cultural shifts and address perennial religious longings.

Paul is also the president and CEO of Goodmakers, an organization dedicated to forming, connecting, and mobilizing leaders for the generational project of cultural renewal.